DATE DUE		

Your essential guide to career success

Second edition

Sheila Pantry OBE
Peter Griffiths

facet publishing

Sheila Pantry OBE is the editor of The Successful LIS Professional Series and author of *Building Community Information Networks: strategies and experiences*, and (with Peter Griffiths) *The Complete Guide to Preparing and Implementing Service Level Agreements*. Peter Griffiths is the author of *Managing Your Internet and Internet Services: the information and library professional's guide to strategy*. Details of these and other Facet Publishing titles are available at www.facetpublishing.co.uk.

Published by
Facet Publishing
7 Ridgmount Street
London WC1E 7AE

Facet Publishing (formerly Library Association Publishing) is wholly owned by CILIP: the Chartered Institute of Library and Information Professionals.

First published as *Your Successful LIS Career: planning your career, CVs, interviews and self-promotion*, 1999
This second edition 2003
Reprinted 2004

British Library Cataloguing in Publication Data
A catalogue record for this book is available from the British Library.
ISBN 1-85604-491-2

Peter Griffiths writes in a personal capacity but is grateful for the Home Office's agreement to the publication of his contribution to this book. Nothing in this text should be taken as an official statement of policy, and mention of any commercial service or product does not imply official endorsement.

Typeset in Aldine 401 and Syntax by Facet Publishing.
Printed and made in Great Britain by Antony Rowe Ltd, Chippenham, Wiltshire.

Contents

Foreword

In the first edition of this book the economy and the job market were both very different from those we are experiencing now, and yet the principles within the book still hold true. In difficult economic times there will be greater numbers of applicants for each job. Your aim should be to submit a quality application that shows you want the job in question and have the skills (or the intention to work to develop the skills) necessary to do it. The recruiters will not be looking for passengers.

It is vital to keep in touch with current job-hunting techniques and to pay more than just lip service to continuing professional development. There is no such thing as a perfect CV or application letter, nor is there a 'standard' form of interview. The minute a CV has been produced it will be out of date. It needs to be examined and checked regularly to make sure it is always an accurate reflection of you and the skills you have to offer.

Keeping abreast of recruitment and selection issues is as important as keeping aware of current developments and issues in LIS. Just as the information society has created the need to add value to information, so must we as information professionals show that we can add value to an organization.

This book is an excellent guide to current thinking and provides an insight into many of the 'behind the scenes' aspects of recruitment and continuing professional development. Dip into it in a quiet moment; take it on holiday and read it cover to cover so that you come back doubly energized; or treat it as a valuable reference tool and refer to it when you need specific help. I will certainly be recommending it to the many candidates that I interview.

Sue Hill MREC HonFCLIP
Managing Director
Sue Hill Recruitment & Services Ltd

1

Scene setting: the challenges of today's employment market

In this chapter we look at:

- challenges of employment changes in the UK, Europe, and internationally
- growth areas for information and library work, such as the finance, legal and medical sectors
- changes and challenges ahead for the library and information professional
- the need to keep up with developments in education and training (continuing professional development) and the skills needed for information and library work, including management skills, web editing skills, language skills, negotiating skills, consulting skills and self-motivation.

Introduction

The first edition of this book provided a much needed guide to the ways that library and information professionals could further their own professional self-development and career in the current job market and to highlight the possibilities to do so. This second edition builds from that by looking at the opportunities that have arisen since then, and showing the range of library and information work now available. It provides guidance on managing every stage of a career, whether you are a young person considering a career in library and information science and wanting to know how to get a foot on the ladder after qualification, a librarian in mid-career, or even a candidate for more senior positions (perhaps with mentoring or careers advisory responsibilities) who wants to get a view of the current state of the profession as a whole. A book of this type cannot deal with all these topics in great detail, but there is an extensive list of information sources to allow the reader to follow up on any point.

In this first chapter we explain the importance of career planning and personal development for librarians and information specialists, and show how career patterns, expectations, and the necessary preparations and actions have changed greatly in a very few years. Later chapters look in more depth at some of the overall issues of career planning and the major events in a career.

We begin with an overview of the current state of the job market and consider the changing skills requirements for jobs with library and information science skills content. Understanding the implications of the ever-growing range of opportunities presents problems for employers and employees. People without traditional librarianship skills are taking on some of the work that was once the preserve of this profession, but librarians are finding their expertise in demand in several new areas of work as businesses and other employers get to grips with the organization and retrieval of the information content of computer and documentation systems.

In Chapter 2 we talk in more detail about the changes that are taking place in the profession and look at a number of employment sectors. These changes present a challenge to the traditional styles of career that many librarians have followed through their entire working lives. Chapter 2 will also show you how to begin planning your career by considering some of the elements that need to be taken into account and suggesting ways to adapt to future changes.

Chapter 3 looks at ways to get a first step on the career ladder, and some of the ways in which you can get practical help at all stages of your career. In the following chapters 4, 5 and 6 we look at the process by which many jobs are filled, taking in turn job advertisements and applications, interview techniques and the paths to further progress. In Chapter 7 we look at how to evaluate job offers and Chapters 8 and 9 cover some of the many other questions you need to consider when planning your career. Chapter 10 gives some career case studies for your information and inspiration, and is followed by appendices and a list of further reading, websites and organizations.

Employment patterns – no more 'jobs for life'?

Many people have discovered that there is no longer any such thing as a completely secure job. You cannot now expect to stay in one job with one employer throughout a career. Many employers are themselves trying to cope with the realities of the current economic situation and you can no longer assume that they will chart a course for you through the organization. In reality, a truly 'glittering' career in information work needs careful planning, and nowadays this falls to you, even if your employer is among the good ones who include career development within their appraisal or personnel management processes. The 'portfolio career' described by Charles Handy (1984, 1995) is fast becoming the norm rather than the exception, especially for those now entering the profession.

On a wider scale, events on the other side of the world can now have a domino effect on jobs in any country. We are still working through the economic effects of the events of September 11, 2001, particularly their effect on multinational organizations, while dealing with the downturn that resulted from the collapse of the Far East economies in 1998. As an information professional you are in a good position to be able to watch the events in the world through various information sources – newspapers, journals, television, radio or internet discussion groups and

3

newsletters – allowing you to track the effect of these events on your own sector of employment or interest regularly. Your job could be changed out of recognition by events over which you have no control, but you can avoid being caught by surprise.

Jobs also disappear. Those information professionals who have worked in the library automation industry, for example, are particularly aware that some of the largest companies, brand leaders of five or ten years ago, have disappeared and their staff have moved on or away. In 2003 a similar process is taking place among subscription agents, with consequences that can be difficult for customers to cope with and disastrous for the staff of the vendors concerned.

Surveys show that the United Kingdom is increasingly developing a long hours culture; even where the issue has been tackled by law, for instance in France, there is a growing feeling that the balance has been tipped too far to enable an effective job to be done. As a result, senior staff are ever more preoccupied with their own jobs and consequently too busy to be able to act as a mentor or guide to less experienced people. Each employee is constantly under pressure to keep the work flowing and to complete it as quickly as possible, often without the benefit of the full picture. Sound advice and development coaching are frequently lacking. The result is a stressed or 'burnt out' individual, without commitment to the employer, and someone who may no longer enjoy the work that previously gave him or her satisfaction.

Today, the customers of our information services have higher expectations than has ever been the case. Even though we warn them against the notion, they believe that the world wide web offers a viable alternative to all our services. As a result they call for professional help far too close to their own deadlines, demand the use of a wider range of information sources and want the results to be delivered in a variety of formats; then they transfer their own pressures onto the information staff. Fortunately, new information and communication technologies (ICT) have also offered information professionals the opportunity to acquire and manipulate information more easily than in the past. But again, they have given the customer the opportunity to channel instant demands that force information professionals to keep abreast of the latest developments in these technologies.

In fact, librarians finally have the opportunities they have been dreaming of for decades as their skills are recognized by the wider world. 'Demand explodes for librarians with high-tech research skills', read the headline to one story on this topic. It went on to state that 'librarians today are hired as "high-tech wizards to navigate the Internet, establish intranets, search databases and classify information"' (Rurak, 1998). The need for computer-literate librarians with 'stellar research skills' continues to grow rapidly. Librarians need to grasp these opportunities (as we pointed out in *Becoming a Successful Intrapreneur* (Pantry and Griffiths, 1998)), but they also need to take these changes into account in considering and planning their future careers.

The effect of official policies

Changes in national and international policies are adding to the challenges that workplace technology has presented to information professionals. Many of the new proposals being put forward in the UK and across Europe will radically alter the way information professionals in these countries work in future. Some of the most important proposals are submitted in the following publications:

- *New Library: the People's Network*, published by the Library and Information Commission in 1997, and the follow-up report
- *Building the New Library*, November 1998
- *The Learning Age: a renaissance for a new Britain*, which included the National Grid for Learning initiative
- The UK government's competitiveness white paper, which includes considerable detail on information and knowledge management issues in the main and supporting papers.

In Europe, issues are raised and opportunities are created for librarians by policies of the European Commission. These include:

- the lifelong learning initiative
- the DigiCult programme, based within the Information Society Directorate, dealing with digital heritage and cultural content
- the e-content programme, which runs until 2005 and includes discussion on the use of and access to public information.

A long-running libraries programme provided a number of opportunities during the 1990s but has now come to an end, at least in its own right. However, a number of EU programmes, particularly the CORDIS research programme, still provide librarians with opportunities in the European context.

These policies are just a few examples of strategies that aim to remove the divide between the information rich and the information poor, reducing social exclusion as well as ensuring the maximum benefit from new information and communication technologies. There are further examples to be found in many countries, all with information as their common baseline, presenting challenges that information professionals and their industry must be constantly ready to accept. If they fail to address these issues, other professions and other sectors will recognize the opportunities and take the lead, leaving the information industry lagging behind.

New focus in subject work

The changes in the employment market generally have led to a concentration in particular sectors nationally and internationally. In this section we look at three areas where there have been marked developments in the library and information field, matching the changes in the industries themselves.

The financial sector

The financial sector is a major producer of information as well as a consumer of it, and provides a number of the most important players in the current information industry. Information is distributed not only via the conventional online databases but also through a variety of other channels. Current financial information is a valuable commodity, but can lose that value in a matter of minutes. Information professionals could find themselves making use of trading systems carrying this valuable real-time data: online databases; the world wide web; or even television, where we have seen the growth of stations dedicated to financial news and comment. The ability to distinguish between good and bad information can make the difference between profit and loss or even lead to the insolvency of a company; the Emulex company suffered great financial damage because false information was relayed by newswire and then by television (Griffiths, 2001, 17).

The legal sector

The legal sector has long provided positions for specialist librarians, and continues to expand. To the growing amount of domestic legislation and the influence of European legislation can be added the need to check the implications of other countries' law-making, for example the effects of the US Patriot Act on the uses of and access to information.

The medical sector

Despite the number of mergers that have taken place in the pharmaceutical industry, there remains an important role for information professionals in the medical sector. Information for healthcare has in contrast grown considerably and continues to do so. In the UK considerable work has taken place in and around the National Health Service, including the development of the NHS Information Authority, the National Electronic Library

7

for Health, and (again, despite the reduction in the number of health authorities) library policies for the National Health Service. The evolution of the discipline of health informatics has added to the opportunities for involvement of library and information professionals.

In addition to these sectors, the growth of the information and communications technologies sector has brought the prospect of further new employment. But not only are there areas of subject specialization where developments have brought new opportunities for library and information professionals, there are also new types of professional work in these and other fields.

New areas of professional work

The intensification of competition now forces many people to move into areas of work in which they may not have had previous experience. Furthermore, new areas of work for library and information specialists are constantly developing, as we saw above and consider again in greater detail later in this book. For example, the focus of many organizations on knowledge management has grown considerably since the first edition of this book. The skills of information and library professionals have been identified as matching exactly what is required to organize, manage, produce and maintain information systems, so that organizations can exploit their own knowledge base more fully. To bring order to the current chaos, they use professional skills such as indexing, thesaurus management and other 'traditional' library techniques. Information technology experts now identify these as necessary skills that are missing from their own strategies for dealing with information overload. Mainstream business literature such as Davenport and Prusak's *Working Knowledge* (1998) sings the praises of librarians at some length. Even if the terminology may be different – suddenly metadata is the fashion – these are simply the latest in a line of such concerns in the business sector about information, knowledge, and the growing volumes of both that are being produced.

Thus you cannot assume that the nature or scope of the profession now remains what it was when you entered it, and still less can you rely on the profession remaining the same throughout whatever length of career you intend to have in future. The pace of change is accelerating. Your choice is to manage your career and adapt to change (and the pace of change), or be sidelined. In an article to which we shall return later, one writer notes that you really cannot start a portfolio career in mid-career – it has to be planned and provided for as soon as possible after qualifying, not least because of the financial and pension planning concerns that arise. But if there is no alternative to changing job, starting your portfolio career is a better option than doing nothing at all.

Working in another country

If you are thinking of working in another country, advice is available from a number of official and other websites. These case studies draw on official websites and on information from the professional organizations in the countries concerned.

Case study 1: Library and information professionals in Canada

Librarians, archivists, conservators and curators
Website: Job Futures (Human Resources Development Canada)
(http://jobfutures.ca/noc/511p3.shtml)
Prospects for this group of occupations are rated fair until 2007. Librarians benefit from above average wages and below average unemployment rates, and have enjoyed growth in prospects because of the private sector's development of corporate archives and memory systems, and the growth of searching on the internet. Government cultural policies are leading to an expansion of library services, and the level of retirements (among the post-war generation) will create a flow of opportunities. This means that although recent graduates will face competition for jobs, the number of jobs

available will broadly match the demand. Candidates with appropriate skills, such as in IT, will have the greatest choice.

Case study 2: Library and information professionals in the United States of America

Department of Labor, Bureau of Labor Statistics
(www.bls.gov/oco/ocos068.htm)

This US government department identifies the use of library automation as an influence that reduces the demand for librarians, moving some formerly professional work to library technicians and giving end-users access to information at the desk top. However, librarians are undertaking more complex and demanding work and, as with Canada, forthcoming retirements will ensure constant job opportunities. Those prepared to work in rural areas have better prospects than those wanting to work in urban areas. Echoing our discussions in other parts of this chapter, the Bureau makes these observations on emerging prospects in new areas of librarianship:

> Non-traditional library settings include information brokers, private corporations, and consulting firms. Many companies are turning to librarians because of their research and organizational skills, and knowledge of computer databases and library automation systems. Librarians can review vast amounts of information and analyze, evaluate, and organize it according to a company's specific needs. Librarians also are hired by organizations to set up information on the Internet. Librarians working in these settings may be classified as systems analysts, database specialists and trainers, webmasters or web developers, or LAN (local area network) coordinators.

Case study 3: Library and information professionals in France

University of Caen
(www.unicaen.fr/unicaen/service/form/centredeformat4/lesmetiers/metiers.
htm)

ADBS (l'Association des Professionels de l'Information et de la Documentation). *L'insertion des jeunes diplômés en information-documentation: promotions 1997–1998, 1998–1999, 1999–2000,* Paris, ADBS, 2002. France is one country where the employment market for librarians and information professionals (often referred to as documentalistes) is highly regulated and structured, with competitions for admission to posts in the public sector, and with some posts in a few government departments reserved for French nationals. However, EU citizens have the right to work in other member countries, and (provided that they meet other requirements, of which fluency in French is usually one) there are ample professional opportunities in France. A survey in 2002 by ADBS, one of France's library and information professional organizations, looked at the progress of three groups of recent graduates. These were some of the findings.

The respondents, who were not all members of a professional body but representative of the profession as a whole, were predominantly female and aged 25–29. In terms of education, 60% had the basic qualification, with two further groups of around 17% each having spent four or five years in higher education. 20% had more than one qualification in information science and 30% of the sample had studied history or the history of art compared with only 11% who had studied scientific subjects. Most of the sample were in work, with only 6% unemployed. Almost one-half of those in work were in the private sector (service industries, banking and insurance being the main sectors) with a further 41% in central or local government, or in public sector companies. Monthly salary levels for this group averaged €1418: interestingly the highest salaries in the survey were paid to those in banking and insurance, but also to the small number of respondents working in the UK. Factors that helped in getting work included qualifications, experience, knowledge of software and fluent English (mentioned by those with the highest level of qualification, where English forms part of the curriculum). When asked which skills they needed to acquire, respondents mentioned website creation skills and project management.

The need for continuing professional development

For any information and library service to function effectively it must have appropriately trained staff. To ensure and maintain this position means first of all that a supply of new information and library professionals with these skills is required. However, it also means that members of the existing workforce must upgrade their skills to meet these new and constant challenges and opportunities in the information industry.

It may surprise information professionals that (discounting students and unemployed or retired members) of the 16,000 personal members of CILIP employed in the UK in 2003 only 5500 work in public libraries. Another 5500 work in academic libraries and information services or schools, with the rest being deployed in a wide range of other organizations, such as financial, legal, consulting, engineering and computing organizations, hospitals, national libraries and government departments or agencies.

It has been said that one Sunday's edition of the *New York Times* today contains more information than a person was exposed to in a lifetime in the seventeenth century.[1] To deal with this, information professionals constantly need to upgrade the variety and depth of their subject skills as well as their professional competences. Without knowledge that is kept constantly abreast of that of the best informed of their customers, information professionals can do no more than run behind those customers and cannot provide a service that continues to play an irreplaceable part in supporting the organization's progress.

Management skills

In the past many information professionals felt that once they had gained their qualifications that was the last major effort they had to make. The wise ones realized that this was only the beginning and planned to ensure their continuing professional development. The development of a graduate profession and the growth of a range of new styles of education and qualifications, such as the Master of Business Administration (MBA) or various courses offered by the Open University, have expanded the range of options available and many librarians have chosen to develop their qualifications and knowledge by pursuing one of them. Management skills are increasingly important as information professionals move through their career, so qualifications such as the MBA have become more popular in recent years. Alternatively, additional specialist skills complement the requirements of library and information work, leading some information professionals to acquire teaching or training skills.

Self-motivation

Whatever you decide about acquiring additional qualifications and skills, including the new skills we discuss below, you will need to develop self-motivation. You may be lucky enough to work for an employer who will sponsor you, or at least provide time off for study; but in many organizations you will in effect be on your own. The motivation that gets you through the course will be your own, or that of yourself and your fellow students. Don't underestimate the effort needed to succeed in study; but the rewards will be the sweet result of your own labour.

New skills for new roles

Web editing skills

As new roles have developed recently for library and information professionals, so these professionals have acquired further skills. Developing web pages is, despite what software vendors would have us believe, not the kind of skill that is acquired in a couple of afternoons as a result of buying a particular web editing package. Creating websites, particularly if these go beyond the most basic functions, is a specialist (and very marketable) skill. A number of librarians have developed the skill levels required, and a few of them have been very successful as a result. The

13

best known example is probably Louis Rosenfeld and Peter Morville. The second edition of their book *Information Architecture for the World Wide Web* (2002) contains a table setting out the differences between libraries and websites, thereby indicating the additional perspectives that librarians need to make a success of working on the web.

Language skills

Language skills are not a new requirement for library and information work, but they have become more important for a number of reasons. The world wide web was originally very much an Anglophone resource. Although estimates vary, the proportion of pages in English on the world wide web at the end of the 1990s was between 50% and 85% (Pimienta, 2000; Internet Society, 1997). However, a 2002 estimate suggested that the proportion of pages in English had by then dropped to 50% (Funredes, 2002). Although many authors write in English for the global market, now other languages – not only Western European languages but Chinese and Russian – have become more important and there is a new demand for the ability to read web pages that are not written in English. It makes sense for the searcher to be able to read other languages, and indeed to be able to use non-English language search engines.

Negotiating skills

In our book on service level agreements (Pantry and Griffiths, 2001) we describe the elements that should appear in these documents and the kind of negotiations that library and information professionals will need to conduct in order to reach these agreements. Negotiating skills are increaisngly important in professional work. Not only are they required when agreeing levels and costs of service, but they are needed in carrying out a range of more senior responsibilities in the library and information service. Negotiating with clients starts with the classic reference interview, which may involve delving below the query presented in order to discover the customer's true requirements. It may involve agreeing deadlines, quality or cost, and the prioritization of work in the library. Those with responsibility for a service or areas such as acquisitions or procurement may negotiate contracts or the supply of services to other organizations (either in the private sector or to some public sector purchasers such as prisons). In another context, those librarians who take a role in collective bargaining or other trades union activities will find these skills very important.

Consulting skills

Information broking and consulting skills are also growing in importance – and not simply for those who now trade on their own as consultants, of which more in Chapter 8. We have remarked before on the increasingly pervasive idea that all knowledge can be found on the internet if only you know where to look. Library and information professionals are only too well aware of the falsehood of this statement, but it needs a well-defined service such as internal consultancy or information broking to bring the point home to many information consumers. Where the librarian acts as a consultant to advise users about their information needs, there is a greater prospect of successful use being made of information resources in order to make business progress.

The demand for new skills does not appear to diminish. As pressure grows in many corporate environments, many business people are finally turning to their library and information professionals for greater support – the support they would have had all along had they made better use of the professional skills of their specialists. But better late than never: we can meet the demand, sometimes simply by using the skills learned during professional education, sometimes using new skills acquired through appropriate training. There is plenty of scope for further development of our profession and its skills.

Summary

In this chapter we have considered:

- changes that have taken place in the employment market for library and information professionals
- the range of work that is now available to information professionals
- the effect of national and international policy on the job market
- new subject areas where employment has become available in recent years and the professional skills required to work in them
- the possibility of working outside your home country
- the importance of continuing professional development and keeping your skills up to date.

NOTE

[1] This assertion is made by Richard Saul Wurman in *Information Anxiety* (1989) and reappears in several forms, involving either the Sunday or weekday edition of the *Times*, and variously a citizen of the Renaissance, the 17th century (Shakespeare is mentioned in some versions) or, strangely precisely considering that this variation turns out to be spurious, 1892. It reappears in *Information Anxiety 2*, by Wurman, Sume and Leifer (2000) in the form of a weekday edition of the *New York Times* and a 17th-century man. Quite how one assertion about information can have spawned so many versions in 15 years is unclear.

2

Your master career plan, or, Do you have to kiss a lot of frogs to find a prince or princess?

In this chapter you will find out:

- how to begin planning your career
- what types of jobs are currently available
- what is happening in the traditional sectors – public, academic and special libraries and information services
- what is happening in other sectors
- what is happening in the 'new' sectors – aggregation which offers new publishing packages, e-publishing, web controllers, media and research.

Do you really have to 'kiss a lot of frogs' to find a prince or princess? In other words, do you have to go continually in and out of jobs to find the one that really suits you at whatever stage of your career? We think not, and show you in this chapter how you can plan your future career – although, as we shall see in a moment, this is not to say that you can necessarily stay in one place for ever.

Over the past five years and since we wrote the first edition of this book there has been a widening of opportunities for the library and information professional in 'new' areas of work. As well as the sectors we described in Chapter 1, these areas include media, research, electronic publishing and 'aggregation', which enables the production of new publishing packages by identifying authoritative sources and bringing them together.

It is essential that you start to plan your career from the outset and continually assess where it is going or should be going. You must be able to take opportunities that come within reach where they suit your career plan. You can do this whether you have qualifications or are still working towards gaining them.

> The . . . librarian is committed to lifelong learning and personal career planning.
>
> [He or she] takes personal responsibility for long-term career planning and seeks opportunities for learning and enrichment. [He or she] maintains a strong sense of self-worth based on the achievement of a balanced set of evolving personal and professional goals.
>
> *Competencies for Special Librarians of the 21st Century* (1996, 2.10)

Job for life or portfolio career?

The idea that a single employer could offer a job for life in library and information work has taken a considerable pounding in recent years. In some cases, service reductions, company mergers or lack of funding has led to a fall in the number of posts and some redundancies. In others, staff have not been replaced and as a consequence the career openings in an organization have been reduced. Younger staff in particular have tired of waiting for 'dead men's shoes' and have gone outside the organization to gain further experience or recognition, and perhaps more rapid promotion.

So, while it is quite common to find that senior staff in larger organizations have worked their way up the system – or at least, that they have spent their career in the same sector – there is a noticeable trend to the 'portfolio careers' of successive frequent job changes that are often found in sectors such as financial services or telecommunications. This trend has advantages and disadvantages for both employer and employee.

Staying with one employer demonstrates commitment but may restrict access to more senior positions as the career pyramid becomes narrower. A study of government librarians in the late 1990s suggested that a range of factors affects the decision to apply (or not) for posts at the most senior levels, particularly whether the additional rewards are worth the extra effort and the challenge of acquiring the post.

As existing senior managers move towards retirement, the trend is in any case to fixed-term appointments – often renewable, it is true – rather than to open-ended appointments. There is likely to be more mobility among the rising generation of senior managers than has been the case until now, and certainly than was the case 30 or 40 years ago. However, there are problems resulting from the departure of senior staff. The employer loses their investment in the individual and also, particularly where the person defects to another employer following some kind of inducement, that person's contacts, knowledge and experience. Given that many libraries have a role in making neutral contact between competing organizations, allowing the mutual and beneficial exchange of information, the loss of the individual librarian's network of contacts can often have a noticeable effect on the organization's competitive capacity.

But constant moves by employees are still seen by many more traditional employers as a sign of insincerity and lack of loyalty, so the prospects for someone constantly on the move may be limited. In some areas these frequent changes might appear as a lack of commitment to the profession itself. The only consolation for an employer is that the short-stay employee will have little time in which to gather intelligence of use to a competitor, but it can cause considerable problems for a project or a team that has been carefully welded together when a team member suddenly decides to move across country or continent.

Recent discussions (which started around pensions issues) about changes to the length of people's working lives are likely to have a longer-term effect on perceptions of this question. If the working career is to be extended to 45 or even 50 years then managerial staff may stay in place far longer, affecting the choice of senior posts on offer as the new rules take effect. And the prospect of a portfolio career lasting up to 25% longer than at present will demand greater planning than many people currently give it.

Risk assessment for jobs

Most people may think that risk assessment is all to do with working safely and healthily, but if you make it part of your everyday thinking and approach to work and life in general, it will provide you with a 'plus and 'minus' list, which you can apply along your career path and which will help you in making other decisions.

Here is a simple risk assessment system with five basic steps – we call it the 'AEIOU model':

1 *Assess*: What are the 'risks' or 'hazards' of the job – e.g. wrong management, wrong location, wrong kind of work for you in the near or middle distance future? Ask your current employer or manager, or their representatives, what they think of your prospects and skills. They may have noticed things that are not immediately obvious.

2 *Evaluate*: Write down your findings (your plus and minus list); your analysis of your future career will help you to decide which way to move. Either stay with the current job and seek opportunities or alternatives within the organization or take the initiative and try pastures new.

3 *Improve*: Can these 'hazards' be improved or eliminated by negotiation – e.g. is it possible to change the terms of the job, so that you can gain some further relevant experience or be helped to obtain further qualifications, or are there any opportunities to work on projects that may give some different type of work experience?

4 *Observe*: Keep the written record for future reference or use; it can help you if you want to move at a later stage in your career. It will also remind

you to keep an eye on particular areas for personal development or jobs that interest you.

5 *Update*: As in all good risk assessment procedures step 5 is to review your assessment from time to time. If your organization has an annual appraisal system then you should revisit and update your plan before each yearly review. It will also show your employer that you are thinking about your career and work in the organization.

Is there a better job for you?

Even excellent jobs are vulnerable to unexpected risks such as the business downturn experienced in 2002 and 2003. However, you can start to decide whether it is time to move to another employer or to devote your energies to improving conditions in your current post by using a simple assessment. Consider the job and its prospects and class them on a simple five point scale as:

Excellent – Good – Fair – Awful – Intolerable

If you rated your job as 'Fair' or worse, you should begin to update your CV, apply for other jobs and attend interviews. If you rate your job as 'Excellent' or 'Good', it may well be worth negotiating better conditions in your present post.

Use this method to rate what you can discover about other jobs against your present one: if you list and mark the elements that are important to you personally (colleagues, training, distance from home, and so on) you can make complex choices much easier by this method.

Getting help

It is often useful to discuss your situation with someone else. This may be someone, whether a professional or not, who when given a snapshot of your current situation is able to help you sort out the possible options available to you. Alternatively, a mentor – either formally within the organization or informally among your circle of professional acquaintances – will maintain a long-term watching brief over your career and be able to apply detailed knowledge of your background to career-related decision-making. In Chapter 3 we look at mentoring in more detail.

So what types of jobs are available?

Wherever there is an active organization you will find there is a need for information services. There are opportunities available in a wide range of sectors – heavy engineering, iron and steel, research, mining, health, government departments and agencies, and public libraries – as well as in consultancy work.

Other areas to consider are electronic publishing, including publicity and marketing, web site creation and maintenance, lecturing, devising training courses, coaching and delivering training. Research is an area that is part of most information professionals' work.

If you are starting out in your career you may decide to gain your first experience in the so-called 'traditional' sector of public and academic libraries.

Public libraries

In the 1990s many public libraries were, sadly, neglected or underfunded. Hours and services were curtailed, bookstocks were reduced and the status of the library in the community declined. Some public libraries took an entrepreneurial approach and expanded their services despite such constraints. Working in these authorities was valuable because it showed how to provide a wide range of public services, despite the need to generate a large percentage of the budget from income – experience that would be valuable throughout your future career. With the publication of

Framework for the Future (United Kingdom, 2003) there may at last be new opportunities for public libraries, and the case studies in the document record some of the good ideas that public libraries have come up with in recent years.

Working in a public library – especially if it is a large public library – offers you opportunities to gain experience in a number of areas – reference work, business information centres, children's libraries, mobile libraries, acquisitions, computer systems including internet web services and general lending library work.

Academic libraries

Working in a university library and information service will give you the opportunity to try out a number of different areas of work – specializing if you wish in certain subject areas, such as engineering or chemistry information. If your first degree is in these subjects then – coupled with your Masters in Information Science – a post working in your specialist area will provide an interesting career. Surveys of available positions show a substantial demand for subject knowledge or experience in professional posts suitable for those at early stages of their careers. Use university and college websites on the internet to check their prospectuses for the range of subjects offered.

If you work in academic libraries you will gain experience in teaching and coaching students, so your presentation skills will need to be improved; perhaps taking a course in these areas will help you.

Education and training sector

As well as universities and colleges, remember that schools, training organizations and business links present opportunities for library and information professionals.

Check directories (see the Further Reading section) that list associations, councils, boards and other bodies, which frequently indicate which have information units. The British Library's *Guide to Libraries and Information Units* (Dale and Wilson, 2003); *Libraries and Information Services in the United Kingdom and the Republic of Ireland* (2003), published by Facet Publishing; and the *Aslib Directory of Information Services in the United Kingdom* (2002) are other useful listings of libraries and information services.

The schools library sector has expanded considerably in recent years, and many schools employ professional librarians with considerable resources at their disposal. These posts are likely to be advertised in local newspapers rather than in the professional press; for a new post the specification may often be rather vague. Experience suggests that when a librarian post becomes available, there will be a detailed and ambitious job specification that reflects the value of the school library to its community.

Work in a training body is likely to either support or form a direct part of the organization's services to its users. As such, this work may have a commercial element to it or at least demand skills in costing and charging for information services. This area of the education and training sector is still developing and opportunities will continue to present themselves. The role of many training bodies in implementing official policies will stimulate their development.

Workplace information and library services

The workplace information and library sector is often overlooked as a career choice by newly qualified professionals. The prospects in this area are considerable, with relevant opportunities no matter what your subject background. Consulting the various directories and handbooks that cover this sector will reveal that many organizations that have an information service.

The satisfaction to be gained working in these specialist areas is enormous – from building and maintaining a one (wo)man service, to running a large department within an organization that could be anything from a blue-chip management consulting firm or financial house to a pharmaceutical or chemical company. There are many opportunities to find interesting information jobs in less obvious industries such as the insurance and loss prevention sector, or the fire information sector.

Health information services merit an entire volume to themselves and can encompass everything from patient libraries at one extreme to the heavy involvement of information professionals in the development of evidence-based practice at the other. The health sector includes the libraries and information services of universities, public sector organizations, charities, hospital libraries, private sector companies and their information services and products, government libraries, and parts of the national libraries.

The development of knowledge management in many corporate workplaces is providing further opportunities for library and information professionals. Working alongside other professionals, and often leading the way, they apply their skills in innovative ways that support people in their workplace to manage the organization's knowledge for the greatest benefit.

Learned societies, professional bodies and charities

Many of the great and long-established institutions provide their members with information services. They include the learned societies and professional bodies in the chemical, civil, structural, fire, electrical and electronic engineering professions; the professional organizations for health and safety practitioners and environment health professionals; the personnel and training institutions; and the registration and professional bodies for a wide range of medical, veterinary and related professions.

Don't forget that many established charities operate information services. Their range of subject coverage is also very wide, and many – from the Consumers' Association to the various overseas development charities – undertake information research in considerable depth. Networking is often a very necessary feature of work in charities.

Government libraries and information services

This is another considerable sector of work opportunities that remains unknown to some library and information professionals. Government departments and agencies offer superb opportunities to gain experience of work in a vast range of areas. Each major department has a library service; the subject matter thus covers agriculture, health, health and safety, trade and industry, defence, communications, economics and finance, foreign affairs, justice, law and order, the environment, transport, taxation, and so on. Changes to the legislative structures in Scotland and Wales have revised the roles of the former Scottish and Welsh Offices, and there has long been a separate departmental structure in Northern Ireland which requires the support of library and information services.

Librarians in central government enjoy an increasing range of jobs, not only in traditional library and information work, but in related areas such as managing and operating helplines and advice services, publishing and publications distribution, website publishing, intranet management, communications (both internal and external), business research and support, legal librarianship, and records and correspondence management. A number of information management and knowledge management roles also exist.

Government librarians have played a major part in the development of metadata standards for the civil service as a whole, and in the continuing development of cross-departmental electronic information services. A long-standing feature of government library work in the UK is posts that are 'outbedded' – that is, librarians work alongside, manage and are managed by generalist or other specialist colleagues but their connection to the departmental or agency library is only through the head of the librarianship profession in the organization. This is information work that is as close to the user as you can get!

We mention work in other countries at various points in this book. It is worth pointing out that, just as in the UK there are some restrictions on nationals of other countries working in some government departments, so there are regulations that may make it difficult or impossible for you to work in the central government sector of some other countries. These regulations may override EU and other regulations. But if your heart is set on some overseas experience it is always worth checking the regulations, because sometimes alternative routes can be found, or an equivalent posting may be available in a department where less strict regulations apply.

Local government offers a little-known type of information work besides public library service in those authorities that employ information and library specialists in their administrative offices. Typical work includes providing information services for council members and officials, supporting the legal department, and maintaining and indexing official archives.

Law

The legal sector offers interesting opportunities for those wishing to work as a non-legal professional in the sector. From university law faculties, government departments to law firms, the information professional will find a range of backgrounds, depending on the specialization of the organization (criminal law, company law, European law, tax law or whatever). A look at the membership of the British and Irish Association of Law Librarians (BIALL), or the European Information Association will show the different types of organizations where suitable and interesting work can be found.

Financial management and consulting houses

The skills of information professionals are increasingly appreciated in the financial management and consulting sectors. The jobs are demanding and exacting but the salaries and other benefits are considerable. Many of these organizations work at the leading edge both in their own work and in that of their clients. Many of the exciting developments in corporate intranets have taken place in the major international consultancy houses. Information is the lifeblood of these consultancy firms and information skills are valued within them. The major consulting and financial houses maintain offices not only in London, but in all the major British cities, including Leeds, Birmingham and Manchester and Edinburgh, in many European financial and political capitals, and in North America, Australasia and the Far East. The business language of most international consultancies is English, but good skills in a second language are useful in this sector.

Publishing sector

Don't forget that the various publishing houses including electronic publishing may also have information services. Library and information skills have further applications in work such as maintaining information-based publications, proofreading and editorial work. Knowledge of fields such as intellectual property, copyright and licensing is valuable here, as in a number of other sectors where it is in demand.

Technology-based jobs

This is where the world is your oyster in that the technologies have not only presented opportunities for new areas of work, for instance in web-related employment, but also offered further opportunities to work in new ways, such as home or distance working, or by taking part in virtual teams and working on a number of different projects simultaneously.

Web work

The information professional contributes a number of activities to web work such as organizing, indexing and retrieving information, which despite new labels (such as 'metadata') are still recognizably core 'traditional' information professional skills. Our experience as users searching for information is also invaluable, as by applying what we learn from searching other people's sites we can improve the navigation and search facilities on our own organization's sites. The fact that we have used technology for so many years in other areas of information work such as database creation and journal control systems makes the transfer into web work a natural step. It is interesting to see how many information professionals in government, health service, legal, finance and other sectors have migrated to web work. If you are entering this area, or are responsible for the delivery and promotion of a successful website and want to make an impact, then Phil Bradley's book *Getting and Staying Noticed on the Web* (2002) will help. For an idea of what is involved in being a webmaster read Chapter 5 of *Managing your Internet and Intranet Services* (Griffiths, 2000).

Many professionals have found that web work has opened up new opportunities, such as working with other parts of their own organizations or running websites. In local government the fact that libraries are often the service with the longest public opening times has of necessity given librarians a higher profile in maintaining the website's operation, in order to keep the library site available at all times.

Electronic publishing

Information professionals are using their skills to produce electronic newsletters and deliver electronic selective dissemination of information to end-users.

Aggregation of quality information sources and producing new commercial packages of information is another exciting area for information specialists. A range of skills – identifying quality information, updating and publishing either in CD-ROM format or via the internet – is needed, and there are new opportunities for information services to earn revenue. See below for opportunities in the traditional book trade.

29

Lecturing, devising training courses, coaching and delivering training

Many information professionals are realizing that their 'traditional' skills in explaining information sources and training users to use these services effectively offer further opportunities for career development. Increasing numbers of people need to access authoritative and validated information, irrespective of time and place, for their own benefit as well as for their organization's requirements. The information professional can play a part and actively develop a new career as a trainer, devising and organizing courses, either with individual clients or more widely, delivering them electronically anywhere in the world.

Library supply: the book and IT trades

The library supply trade employs a number of professional librarians. They may be recruited for their ability to verify information supplied by customers for publications or to maintain corporate information databases for book supply houses and publishers, where managers have found it cost-effective to bring librarians onto their teams to liaise with library customers and to check the more obscure publication references. Those with information technology skills can find work as sales or support staff with library computer suppliers, having regular contact with customers, providing training, or helping to deal with problems.

If you have editorial skills, you may find work writing technical manuals or sales proposals. The traditional book trade continues to offer a range of opportunities; skills such as proofreading can be useful – as well, perhaps, as negotiation and other skills less associated with librarians. We discussed the possibilities in the growing sector of electronic publishing above.

Joining associated groups

It is worth joining the various groups of the UK's Chartered Institute of Library and Information Professionals (CILIP), international information and library professional bodies such as the Special Libraries Association, or those of other countries to find out more about what work is available in various sectors. You can attend meetings, go on visits to the information centres and libraries of various organizations, and receive newsletters and other information which will widen your knowledge of the opportunities available. The same applies if your current employer is a member of an Aslib group. You may well read about or visit an information service that you would like to join, and can save valuable time and effort by focusing your job searching on organizations with which you are already familiar through visits or reading.

There are also a number of specific subject groups. For example, the UK Fire Information Group is linked to the International Fire Information and Research Exchange (inFIRE), which in turn can lead you to information careers in this specialist area. Some of the fire information services represented in these groups have backgrounds ranging from private consulting engineering companies, the academic sector, fire brigades and government departments to training colleges.

Taking a worldwide approach

Of course these opportunities do not stop at the frontiers or shoreline of your country.

In a guide such as this, we cannot cover the requirements for working in other countries in any detail. As a general rule, if you are a citizen of a member country of the European Union you can find work within the EU in similar organizations to those that we have described above. Your UK qualifications will generally be recognized (although their equivalence to other national standards will vary from country to country) under the directives on the equivalence of professional qualifications. However, just as in the UK, certain posts (for example in some government departments) may be restricted to nationals of the host country. You should check carefully before investing time and energy (and particularly travel expenses) in seeking work abroad. But for the right candidate a period working in another country's professional environment can give an advantage in seeking future positions that will last throughout their further career.

If you have a good second European language, there are considerable opportunities available; even if your language skills are moderate, there are still posts available in some international organizations and colleges where the working language is English. We carried out a survey of opportunities in France for the first edition of this book, and we have now followed this up at the end of Chapter 4 to see how things have changed since then.

The Special Libraries Association's *Competencies for Special Librarians of the 21st Century* (1996) describes the skills that are considered essential in North America and other areas of the world where the American influence is strong. These are not explicitly ranked, but among the major professional skills identified are (once again) knowledge of database and information source content, subject knowledge, customer-related skills including training, and use of information technology; among personal qualities, communications skills, team-working skills and flexibility are important.

It pays to research your target country's job market. If you decide to try for work in another country on your own account rather than through an exchange bureau, the best route is to contact one of the professional organizations in the country you are considering working in. Some UK organizations have links with their counterparts elsewhere (through bodies such as the European Bureau of Library, Information and Documentation Associations (EBLIDA) or the European Council of Information Associations (ECIA); you could check with organizations such as the International Federation of Library Associations (IFLA) or the British Council, which has offices throughout the world, or you could discover from one of the other international professional bodies who their national member organizations are. Alternatively – as we suggest elsewhere – simply write to the personnel department of any organization where you especially wish to work.

A number of websites are available that list job vacancies in particular countries, but the rub is that you may need to be a member of the national professional society to get a password for the vacancy advertisements. Others such as the American Library Association site are open to all comers but there is a growing trend to 'lock' parts of websites for members' use only. Before you apply for anything, check your eligibility for the work, for residence, and for visas and work permits. Contact the relevant foreign embassy or High Commission in your own country for help.

Summary

After reading this chapter you should have a good idea of:

- how the nature of work has changed from jobs for life to portfolio careers
- how to assess your current position and decide whether to move on
- where jobs are currently to be found
- whether your skills are transferable to other countries.

3

Starting your career

This chapter looks at:

*   the growing opportunities for people with library and information quali-
    fications
*   researching the marketplace
*   what to think about when looking for a job.

But even if you are well into your career, there is something in this chapter for you. The market has changed greatly in a few short years and there
may be new opportunities to use your skills. It is never too late to plan
your next move and the tips here are as useful for people seeking career
change as they are for the new entrant to the profession.

Some people do not plan their careers; they may be successful despite
a total lack of planning or real interest in finding their next job. However,
most people need to spend some time planning and reviewing their careers.
For a newcomer to the profession the first step, even before taking any
qualifications, is to find out what type of work is available, and what might
appeal to you. Use this information in selecting the courses that you apply

for in order to get your professional training and qualification.

In Chapter 2 we provided an overview of the vast range of possible backgrounds that can offer interesting careers in libraries and information centres. Now we look from the other direction to identify the growing range of types of work that library and information professionals undertake.

'Conventional' library and information work

We put the term 'conventional' in quotes because there is increasingly less convention and tradition in the field. There are certainly still some areas where skills in handling traditional materials – particularly older books and documents, and their catalogues – are at a premium. The daily work of many librarians is a mix of tasks based on printed and electronic sources; library and information work relies more heavily than ever on core disciplines such as cataloguing and classification, and on document retrieval and delivery. Even if the terminology now uses words like metadata and resource discovery, the skills involved are recognizably the same. But in recent years a host of new fields has developed where library and information professionals can find satisfying work.

New areas of work for library and information professionals

Whatever view you take of where 'conventional' library and information works starts and finishes, there is no doubt that many new kinds of job opportunities for people with library and information professional qualifications have been created in a few years. The kinds of work described below can be found in many countries, and make up a growing proportion of the posts available.

Web work

The growth of the internet, and especially the world wide web, has given rise to a wide range of opportunities for the library professional. Librarians played an important role during the mid-1990s in developing and popularizing search facilities as the web developed. This has paved the way for their natural involvement in the creation of websites and pages. In many cases they act as web authors or editors; a number of library websites provide their users with resource guides while others form part of a local authority or other larger site where people with information skills arrange, index and maintain the site. Time and again it is librarians' understanding of the ways that people search for and retrieve information that makes their contribution to a website valuable.

Resource centres

Convergence – the bringing together of linked services such as libraries and information technology into a single management structure – has created a number of opportunities for library and information professionals. One of these is in the specialism of library systems work, which has long been pursued by librarians with an interest in and an aptitude for technology. Another more recent form of convergence is in the growth of learning resource centres where a range of educational technologies are managed alongside more conventional library resources. There is often a tutoring role (perhaps harking back to the tutor-librarian role in colleges during the 1980s and 1990s) with librarians training people in how to use the various software packages and audiovisual materials. In some centres, the skills that librarians need may be rather different from those traditionally required and candidates will need to acquire additional experience or training before taking on this kind of work. A typical post could have a range of duties such as induction for new students, supporting them as their courses progress, and obtaining the resources needed to develop the service. There could be opportunities to get involved in leading-edge technical developments such as virtual learning environments and other online learning innovations. A frequent requirement for posts of this type is up-to-date knowledge of information and learning technologies (ILT), so you should be prepared to develop an in-depth understanding of this area if you decide to go in this career direction.

Reading or literacy development: Sure Start and other projects

The development of literacy in children – and in adults – is a key theme in modern society. People who cannot cope with reading the vast range of material that we all encounter every day are at a distinct disadvantage. The development of literacy is a specialized but rewarding area of work that is attractive to many actual or would-be library and information professionals. The government places considerable emphasis on literacy as part of its education policy.

Among the policy initiatives that have created a number of opportunities for library and information professionals is Sure Start, which combines elements of childcare, education, healthcare and family support in a single strategy. This government policy involves helping young children through the foundation stage of the National Curriculum, and has information service elements for children (at a local level) and parents (at a national level). A further initiative, Bookstart, has been in operation through a trust since 1992 and encourages book ownership by very young children. It too operates in connection with healthcare services but it is generally library professionals who manage the many local schemes. Some recent job advertisements have linked Sure Start and Bookstart activities in a single post. Useful interests or knowledge for this area would include knowledge or awareness of social exclusion issues, child development and working alongside families. Community language skills are a further advantage in this area of work.

Subject specific services

Some areas of subject specialization may be fairly obvious. In many public library authorities there will be one or more music specialists and many university librarians have a subject specialism in addition to their library professional skills. Information science as a discipline grew out of the needs of scientific and technical companies for a specialized form of librarianship that included in-depth subject knowledge and expertise as well as the skills of document sourcing and management. This requirement for subject expertise continues today; while some subject fields such as law are obvious areas for librarians with subject specialist knowledge to work in, many of the sectors that first employed information scientists continue to need people who can combine subject knowledge with library and information skills. Degrees in life sciences or chemistry continue to be sought by a number of employers. There are many posts for information professionals in healthcare and those with suitable clinical knowledge can move into areas such as medical informatics. Another area where subject specialist skills are required is careers information services.

Research and analysis

Those who have specialist skills in information retrieval may be able to work in the various fields of research. With increasing emphasis on the use of evidence in a range of subject disciplines – once again, starting from work done in the field of healthcare in the early 1990s – there are opportunities for library and information professionals to play an important role in identifying and gathering evidence from existing studies and presenting it to research teams. For those with skills of review and analysis, there are further opportunities to carry out the actual analysis of the retrieved data and other evidence. Frequently this role combines subject knowledge with information skills.

Competitive intelligence

Closely related to research and analysis is the field of competitive intelligence. One leading organization describes it as 'the legal and ethical collection and analysis of information regarding the capabilities, vulnerabilities, and intentions of business competitors' (SCIP, n.d.). Competitive intelligence focuses on the activities of competing organizations, seeking to find information that will disclose from public sources both what the competitor plans to do and what the competitor is saying about competing organizations. These obviously include the company employing the information analyst but may include the subjects of other competitor analyses. This is an exciting field to work in, which some argue is becoming a professional discipline in its own right. It is better developed in some other countries than the UK (the USA and France are two leading exponents, so language skills can be important in getting work in the field).

Knowledge management

There will be considerable discussion for some time to come over the exact difference between information management and knowledge management (KM), but it is enough for our purposes to note that the growth of KM has produced a number of new jobs, often at comparatively senior levels in the employing organizations. This is an area where a number of professions, not least experts in information and communications technology, have staked a claim; but with their understanding of the use of information as well as its structures and organization, librarians have a considerable impact. Thomas Davenport and Laurence Prusak, two of the most important contributors to the development of this field, speak of the need for managers who 'come from a background that emphasizes the creation, distribution or use of knowledge . . . organizations need people who will extract knowledge from those who have it, put it in structured form and maintain or refine it over time. Universities don't really teach these skills but the closest approximation is found in journalism and library-science curricula' (Davenport and Prusak, 1998, 112, 110).

The book trade

The publishing and bookselling trade has a range of opportunities for library and information professionals. Publishing offers the possibility of bringing knowledge and experience of information products to the editorial team, and offers prospects of taking managerial or financial responsibility for a printed or electronic product that will be used by libraries and others. Apart from editorial posts, there are jobs in taxonomy and the organization of published information, research for new publications, and involvement in the entire publishing process. The bookselling trade has employed librarians for some years, primarily to support customers through bibliographic checking services that check customer-supplied details and support those customers without ready access to professional librarians.

So there is ample scope for using library and information qualifications even if you never work in what people might regard as a conventional library! Now that you have seen the widening range of work available, how do you start to make your career? This is how we suggest that you go about it.

Research the marketplace

If you are still at school and considering a career in library and information work you should start with a visit to your local careers library. Ask your careers adviser to give you more information about the opportunities in some of the wide variety of backgrounds that we mentioned above. Some of the possibilities we described are very new, and you may need to do some searching for yourself with the help of your careers adviser.

It may be possible for you to visit some of the information centres and libraries that operate in various subject areas. Find out if there are specialist groups of people working in the subject of your choice. In the UK, many of these groups are special interest groups of the Chartered Institute of Library and Information Professionals (CILIP). There are also a number of independent groups such as the Circle of State Librarians (for those working in UK government departments and agencies), the Association of Information Officers in the Pharmaceutical Industry (AIOPI), the Association of UK Media Librarians (AUKML) (for those in libraries serving newspaper and broadcasting organizations), and so on. Some addresses are given at the end of this chapter and many of the organizations have websites that give details of their activities as well as contact information.

There are many ways in which you can gain an insight into the workings of a library and information service. You may for example find temporary employment in a suitable local service. Watch for advertisements in the local press, or call or write to one that interests you, offering your services. Some of them may be able to take you for work experience, or for a placement (paid or unpaid) during a holiday period. Use the directories of libraries listed at the end of this book to identify possible employers.

Qualifications

The academic qualifications needed to be able to work at a professional level in the information industry are:

- a first degree in library and information science (or a similarly named discipline)
- a first degree in your chosen subject plus a second academic qualification in library and information science – which can be a postgraduate diploma or a Master's degree from a recognized school of information science or librarianship.

The next step in becoming a fully qualified information professional is to work towards Chartered Membership of CILIP.

With the merger of The Library Association and the Institute of

Information Scientists to become CILIP, people who held an ALA or MInfSc now hold the postnominal MCLIP (Chartered Member) to denote their professional qualification. (A number of Members will progress to Fellowship, the qualification that CILIP bestows for longer and more distinguished contributions to the profession, as did the predecessor organizations.) Candidates for Chartership present evidence of professional maturity gained since acquiring their academic qualifications by presenting a portfolio of evidence after a qualifying period. A new qualification structure is being developed, which will also address the question of recognition of work-based professional experience and a wider range of entry into the Chartership process. The new structure will come into force in early 2005.

Courses

You should check that CILIP has accredited the institution where you want to study and the course you want to take in information and library science. CILIP checks the quality and content of the courses on offer and accredits courses (or sometimes individual modules within courses) as meeting its standards and the requirements of the profession. Although there is no implication that the courses without accreditation are in some way inferior, you may find that those employers with a strict policy on the level of qualification for employment (and this includes the UK government) will give preference to those whose courses were fully accredited by CILIP.

There are a number of schools of information studies in the UK in a wide range of locations, from Aberdeen, Edinburgh and Glasgow in Scotland, to Aberystwyth in Wales, and Birmingham, Brighton, Bristol, Leeds, Liverpool, London, Loughborough, Manchester, Newcastle and Sheffield in England.

If you have a subject degree, working in a library or information service for a period will provide valuable experience before you go on to take your diploma or masters degree in information science. Suitable posts for those intending to take postgraduate qualifications are often advertised in the professional press and may appear locally. Even if you do not return to your degree subject after postgraduate study, this kind of experience will add to your future employability.

Studying abroad

Similar structures exist in education for library and information science in Europe, North America and elsewhere. If you have connections to another country that would allow you to study there (and bear in mind that EU citizens have wide-ranging rights to travel and study in other countries within the Union) then this could be a possibility for you. CILIP recognizes the qualifications of a number of other library and information associations and will give advice. And if you intend to spend part of your career in a particular country then it could make sense to hold a qualification from that country. Again, qualifications are supposed to be transferable within the EU but bear in mind that patterns of study may be different in other countries and that your UK (or other country's) qualification may not represent the same number of years of post-school study as the local qualification does.

What are and where are the jobs?

To find out what types of job exist one of the best ways is to check the various advertisements that appear in CILIP's *Library and Information Appointments*, issued fortnightly to members. (This will be replaced by a revamped CILIP fortnightly bulletin including job vacancies, which will probably be launched in early 2004.) In *Appointments*, also available on the internet, and other bulletins you will find jobs advertised from a wide range of organizations:

- universities and colleges
- public libraries
- schools
- medical information services including the National Health Service
- research organizations

43

- learned institutions
- charities
- commercial, industrial and business companies
- technical and scientific institutes
- government departments and agencies
- local government departments – that is, areas of local government other than public libraries.

Other advertisements appear in professional journals and newsletters. We discuss them in more detail below.

There are a number of recruitment services (see our suggestions listed at the end of the book) that will also give you good advice on the types of job on offer and the qualifications needed. Some will also give advice and suggest the type of training needed for certain jobs. Whichever path you choose, you will need your professional qualifications together with:

- information technology skills – awareness, literacy
- good interpersonal skills
- good presentational skills.

The professional bodies

Quite apart from the standard benefits of membership that we mention from time to time in this book, professional organizations offer you some excellent opportunities to develop your career through becoming fully involved in their activities. These all depend on some kind of voluntary input, but they provide contacts, experience of working in teams and committees, experience of working with professional colleagues from other sectors and types of information and library services, and some exposure to the realities of commercial life if you work in the public sector. Information professionals benefit from involvement with their colleagues in a way that few other professional people do. This skill in networking has been one of the factors that has led corporate and public managements finally to recognize the value of their librarians and information professionals in new disciplines such as knowledge management.

Getting involved with one of the professional organizations is probably the most significant contribution you can make to your own career. If your employer already provides time during working hours for this activity, take advantage. If not, ask whether it is possible, and if the answer is still no, work out how much (or how little) it would cost you to devote one evening a month to your own career development. Then pick up that telephone and ask how you can get involved!

The current contact addresses for a range of the professional bodies and a note of some of their sub-groups are given in the notes for this chapter. The creation of CILIP from The Library Association and the Institute of Information Scientists has been a catalyst for a realignment of these sub-groups; some former special interest groups are now independent, while other formerly independent groups are interested in becoming part of the CILIP structure. Branches are being reorganized with new geographic boundaries that coincide with the government's development areas.

Specialist work

There are specialist groups working in many subject areas of librarianship. They include special interest groups of CILIP as well as some independent bodies. Aslib, which has personal student membership, but is primarily an organization whose members are companies and corporate organizations, has a number of special interest groups based on industry sectors. They provide careers information suitable for school leavers as well as for new graduates and other university-level entrants to the profession. A number of specialist organizations serve particular types of library or subject field. These include the Circle of State Librarians (for those working in information centres and libraries of government departments and agencies), the British and Irish Association of Law Librarians (BIALL), the Association of Information Officers in the Pharmaceutical Industry

(AIOPI), the Association of UK Media Librarians (AUKML), and IFM Healthcare, a sub-group of the Health Libraries Group of CILIP, which focuses on information to support the management group in the National Health Service.

Where do I find out about available jobs?
Advertisements

Many advertisements for suitable posts appear in the obvious places, that is the vacancy publications issued by the professional bodies in the library and information fields listed in the references to this chapter. However, probably as a result of the publishing strikes in the Times group of newspapers in the 1980s, which prevented the printing of library job advertisements in the *Times Literary Supplement*, a range of other publications now carry advertisements for jobs in this field. The content of the publication may reflect the type of post; for example, the *Guardian* media supplement has advertisements for jobs in publishing, newspapers and broadcasting and the society supplement carries those for other areas of the public sector; the *Times Educational Supplement* and *Higher Education Supplement* carry advertisements for posts in schools, colleges and universities, and specialist trade magazines take advertisements for their own sectors. Trade journals frequently carry vacancy notices too; for example the *Health Service Journal* frequently advertises jobs in health libraries in the NHS and elsewhere in the sector. Advertisements for some of the non-traditional posts appear in *New Media Age* (for web-related posts). It is worth remembering that personnel departments often do not know which publications carry library job advertisements, so an organization advertising a newly created librarian post may well restrict the advertisement to its own specialist trade press more out of lack of awareness than from any desire to restrict applications.

One of the best ways to find out what types of job exist is to check the various advertisements that appear in CILIP's *Library and Information*

Appointments, which is issued twice a month to members and is also available on the internet through the CILIP website. Jobs are advertised by a wide range of organizations, so opportunities in all the types of library listed in Chapter 2 will probably occur over a short period. Other advertisements appear in professional journals and newsletters, for example in *Information World Review*, published by VNU Business Publications, as well as various newspapers. There are a number of web-based recruitment services and posts are frequently advertised on the mailing and discussion lists operated by Jiscmail such as lis-link.

Employment agencies

You might also decide to apply for a job through an employment agency. A number of recruitment services and agencies specialize in posts in information and library services, and in a range of related work such as information management and knowledge management. The list of references associated with this chapter shows many of the agencies in the UK. In a number of cases the agencies pre-screen candidates and then match and provide job seekers' details to prospective employers against job profiles. Some of these recruitment services will also give advice on the types of training, qualification and skill that are needed for certain types of job, and advise on the range of posts and work available.

The generalist

Despite all we have said, you may find it difficult to choose a sector in which to work. In this case, you may do best to stay a generalist and choose posts accordingly. At the beginning of your career, public libraries can offer a wide range of work including dealing with business enquiries, music, local studies and children, as well as the traditional adult lending and reference services. Generalist work is sometimes available in surprising places. For example, the UK's Ministry of Defence operates some libraries for service personnel and their families serving at bases outside the UK and many public library authorities operate service points within prisons, sometimes integrated with their own services, sometimes semi-autonomous, that offer library and information services to inmates. Generalist skills can, by definition, be applied in a wide range of situations and the choice of posts available to non-specialists may finally be as wide as your imagination and enthusiasm allow it to be.

Experience: how long is long enough?

We all know people who say they have ten years' experience, but is it really ten years of experience, or one year's experience times ten? Those further on in a career will benefit from a change of work or job at three- to four-year intervals. (A year to learn a job, a year to do it well, a year to improve it and a year to get stale and find another job?) Too short a time and it is impossible to show any achievement or progress; too long a time and it looks like lack of ambition.

Some employers attempt to manage their employees' career development by rotating people and posts at regular intervals. However, it is quite difficult to do this at all effectively where there are very few librarians, or where there are only one or two posts on comparable levels. In this respect, some of the large universities, public libraries and industrial libraries score well. Conversely, with increasing specialism in areas of work such as internet editing (HTML coding and so on), people are less willing to leave posts that keep them at the leading edge of their specialism, and employers are less willing to lose staff with these skills, which have often been provided through expensive training.

You may consider staying with an organization for a second three- to four-year period if the job changes significantly or there are opportunities to learn other skills. An employer may assist staff's personal development by offering, for example, facilities to gain a further qualification such as an MBA, in order to retain the services of an experienced employee. The real question for the employee is whether he or she is gaining any more real and valuable experience by staying.

Work patterns

Other work patterns that may help both employer and employee to resolve some of these issues are also emerging. It is becoming more common for people to have two jobs, or to carry out their work on more than one site. (We shall be saying more in later chapters about related questions such as working from home and career breaks.) It is often possible to combine two or more part-time posts to make a full-time working week. Providing that the law on working hours (based around an EU directive) is not breached, the employee is clearly at liberty to combine posts into a longer week than a single employer might have provided. Such arrangements may provide a range of experience somewhat faster than a single job can. However a potential employer would no doubt wish to ensure that there was no conflict of interest between his or her needs and those of the second employer and may place restrictions on other work, especially work intended to supplement a full time job.

Consideration of other factors, such as family responsibilities, are going to have an important effect on the sort of hours you will be able to work. The literature suggests that working non-standard hours makes many people feel exposed ('are they doing this as a favour?'), but it is worth bearing in mind that in some areas of the profession there is no such thing as a standard working day because the norm is to work shifts with days off midweek, when the library is often closed anyway. The nature of information work is also changing as the trend to 24/7 working – 24 hours a day, seven days a week – continues to grow. Multinational companies and their information services, as well as some universities, now work round the clock, so there are already a few opportunities for working at unusual times and these are likely to grow. Even the trend in public libraries to weekend opening brings further opportunities to gain different experience as well as financial rewards. In coming to decisions on issues like these a second opinion is often helpful. As we have already mentioned, a mentor can help you by providing advice of this kind.

Mentoring

Mentoring is an important activity that is often mentioned in connection with the career development of library and information professionals. Mentoring suits the profession well, and has particular benefit where a librarian or information officer is working in a small or one-person unit without access to other professionals in the organization. It allows a person to receive the benefit not only of the experience of someone else, but also of that person's experience in different sectors of information work. But what exactly is mentoring, and how do you set about doing it?

The definitions of mentoring vary. Research suggests a variety of approaches to the process depending on the country in which it is taking place. In the UK there may be more emphasis on learning and coaching, and less on sponsoring a person's entire career (which might, in the wrong circumstances, be construed as nepotism). Whatever else it is, mentoring usually means the development of someone – usually younger and probably not within the same area of a management chain – who is less experienced in the profession than the mentor. However, there is no 'right' or 'wrong' way to go about the process, as we shall see in the rest of this section.

A mentor is described as a trusted counsellor, guide, tutor or coach. (The term comes from the name of the friend of Odysseus to whom the education of Odysseus' son Telemachus was entrusted in *The Odyssey*.) The modern sense of mentoring includes supporting and sometimes actively coaching a student in his or her learning, together with the idea of encouraging or even sponsoring and promoting the student within the organization or the profession. The rather ugly term 'mentee' is found, meaning the person mentored, but the words 'protégé', 'learner' or 'pupil' are increasingly used. Mentoring at its most effective ought to be a two-way process, so that the older person also gains benefit from learning about new developments and other points of view from younger members of the profession. It therefore benefits both parties and is good for the profession as it promotes a flow of ideas across the generations.

The relationship can be more or less formal, ranging, for example, from occasional telephone discussions or lunch-time meetings to more formal regularly scheduled meetings, probably in the mentor's office and workplace. Each of these styles has its advantages, with the more formal style probably approaching that of a university tutorial session. This is more often found where an organization operates a formal programme of mentoring or personal development.

UK literature on the subject is in broad agreement about the features of mentoring. The summaries below reflect that tradition. Those interested in further aspects of mentoring would find it useful to read some US or other non-UK documents.

Some of the key elements of the mentoring relationship, according to UK tradition, are listed below. Mentoring should be:

- non-threatening and non-judgmental
- wider in scope than simply providing professional advice
- a long-term commitment or agreement (but this is not to say that a mentor–pupil relationship that has run its course should not be replaced by another, or that either party can no longer take part in a useful mentoring relationship with other people)
- a commitment of time and energy by both parties
- an expression of mutual respect
- an introduction to other networks of people and influence.

Some of the elements of the mentor's job are to:

- manage the relationship – including making time for the pupil despite existing commitments
- encourage and motivate, and to provide feedback – to teach and to nurture

51

- respect the pupil and his or her views, even when you disagree with them
- be responsive to the pupil
- consider how to provide a role model
- demonstrate skills for the pupil to emulate
- defend the pupil and provide emotional support where appropriate.

Some of the elements of the pupil's task are to:

- communicate ideas and reactions back to the mentor, failures as well as successes, and to discuss forthcoming areas of learning or development with the mentor
- respect the views and advice of the mentor, even when you disagree with them
- manage the relationship, including making time for the mentor and keeping to agreed appointments
- keep interested parties aware of the relationship, within the bounds of confidentiality agreed with the mentor (this is especially important where the mentor is in a different management chain or even a different organization)
- listen, particularly when the mentor is offering advice gained from his or her own experience on the avoidance of pitfalls.

Mentoring is a common and very valuable activity in information and library work. There are no formal programmes within the profession but many larger organizations have general schemes, and they can be found in other workplaces such as local authorities and public services. Some companies use mentoring as part of their general staff development. Consider whether your mentor need be a librarian at all. You could learn much, and also give much in return, if your mentor were a generalist manager, or a specialist in some other discipline.

The traditional networks that librarians and information specialists use to communicate provide the source for many mentoring partnerships. In a profession where there are so many small organizations and solo professionals within larger organizations, the contacts made at training courses, social events and meetings such as the members' days run by the various professional bodies are essential for professional development and to facilitate mentoring. Biddy Fisher's book *Mentoring* (1994), published by Library Association Publishing, looks at mentoring from the particular viewpoint of libraries.

Deciding what is right for you

Go back to Chapter 2 to help you decide what is right for you, then you can start to make your plans accordingly and discuss with your mentor and other professional organizations as we have suggested above.

Summary

After reading this chapter you should know:

- what are the areas with new opportunities in professional work
- how to find out about the different types of library where you could work
- what professional qualifications are available, and how to start gathering information on how you obtain them in the UK
- where to find recruitment agencies, advertisements and advice
- when to consider moving on
- how a mentor could help you.

4

Applying for a job

In this chapter we consider how to go about finding a job from advertisements, and other ways of seeking to enter the job market. We cover:

- how to find out about an organization and decide whether to apply
- whether to take a temporary post
- how to write an application letter and put together a CV
- competences – what are they and what use are they in job applications?
- when to apply 'cold' for a job – the unsolicited job application.

How to read a job advertisement

We looked in Chapter 2 at the range of work that is now opening up for people with library and information science training, and in Chapter 3 at the places where you can find job advertisements. Remember that many jobs are never advertised in the press. Sometimes people are head-hunted, that is, they are approached and asked if they would be interested in a particular job and then asked to go for an interview. This type of activity will be found mainly in the private sector, both in the UK and around the world.

It is already apparent that many suitable posts for librarians will not have the word 'library' or 'librarian' in the job title. It pays more than ever to begin with an open mind, and to read advertisements with the thought in mind: 'How do my LIS skills map onto the requirements of this post?'

Job advertisements should give you two sorts of information: first about the job being offered and second about the organization. Sometimes you can glean as much from what the organization doesn't say, or how it says what it does, as from what it wants to tell you. Sometimes events have a way of catching up with an advertisement. A company may include a line about how well it is doing, when the newspaper stories say it has decided to lay off half its employees. A public sector body may be about to contract out its library. Each may still be a good place for a dynamic librarian to work, but it pays you to read around your application.

Most employers will describe a post in glowing terms and there will probably be an information pack or at least a more detailed job description that sets them out in detail. There will often be a number of well-intentioned statements that declare the library to be some kind of paragon and the post to be vitally important in the structure. If this is accompanied by a salary range that appears miserly in relation to the effort and skills demanded, it may be a sign of a future problem. It may be quite an acceptable post for gaining experience but not for any long-term future.

However you find your job vacancy, use the same basic technique when considering whether to apply for it.

Whether to apply for a post

The changes that we described in Chapter 1 have opened up a wide range of posts to librarians. Similarly, as a glance at the recruitment newsletters will readily show, there is progression and promotion, and a good number of vacancies for qualified and qualifying information and library professionals is advertised in an average month. So the choice is wide, and all the reader need do is select the best paid posts and apply for them.

Or is it as simple as that? Ask what position the job you identify will play in your career plan. Will it give you a skill you currently lack? Will it allow you to develop in a subject area you want to work in? Will it provide the next step on the ladder in your chosen area of work? Is the company name of the employer going to make your future job applications look better? Or is it just a well-paid dead-end?

Salary will certainly be important, and if you are willing to take a salary cut to work in a particular library, you must consider the consequences carefully. (The interviewers will almost certainly remark on this, so think before you apply.) Fringe benefits may, if paid, make up for a salary drop. On the other hand, you may find the amount of pension contributions you now have to make has changed. You may also be able to negotiate other benefits such as having some further training course(s) paid for. Make sure you know what financial difference there will be overall if you are successful – and therefore what your bargaining points are if you have to negotiate on pay as part of the job offer when you are selected.

You need to do a full 'plus' and 'minus' assessment of what the benefits are going to be in the long term.

Do your homework

Find out enough about the organization to know that you want to apply. As a library and information professional you are in a good position to find material about any potential employer. Read what it says in the advertisement, and see how the organization sells itself. Find its annual report and any other publications that are available, and see what they add to your knowledge of the organization and how this tallies with the information given in the advertisement. If you can read a balance sheet, how is your prospective employer doing? What does the press say? Is there anything on the internet such as an organizational website? (Sometimes the opponents of the organization may have a website as well.)

If the organization manufactures something, look at its range of prod-

ucts. If it has a well-known person in charge as chairman, managing director, or whatever, find out about that person.

It will be beneficial to your application if you are informed about the
organization with whom you are being interviewed for a job. We have
interviewed many people who simply did not know anything about the
organization with whom they had applied to work. So much for their information skills!

You need to be aware of a number of other details about the organization in question, which may not be in the advert or apparent from
research or on their web pages. For example:

- Are flexible working hours available?
- Is it a non-smoking environment? This is useful to know if you suffer from smoky atmospheres; or if you are a smoker you will want to
  know the conditions in which you may smoke, e.g. is a smoking room
  available?
- If the advert says 'good working conditions', exactly what does this mean?
  For instance, is there a staff cafeteria, ergonomic furniture and up-to-
  date IT equipment?
- Are there implications of the Disability Discrimination Act (DDA) that
  affect you?

The result of this research will also allow you to give confident answers to
interview questions such as 'Why do you want to work for us?' and 'What
contribution can you make to this organization?' You will also become aware
of any current issues that the interviewer may ask you about – or be able
to steer the conversation round to show your awareness of them!

Equal opportunities

At recruitment and selection stage, employers need to consider how the
implications of the DDA affect the:

- job description and person specification
- advertisement and application forms
- short listing of applicants
- invitation to interview
- health and medical checks
- induction and training of staff
- access to buildings.

There are a number of government services aimed at improving employment options for people with a physical disability. Some disability charities have also developed employment services. Measures that might be taken include:

- transferring the person with a physical disability to fill an existing vacancy
- altering someone's hours of work
- acquiring special equipment or modifying existing equipment
- giving special induction and training for staff with physical disabilities
- improving access to buildings
- making other adaptations to premises.

The Chartered Institute of Library and Information Professionals has an 'Equal Opportunities Briefing on the Employment of Disabled People in Library and Information Services'. This is available on the CILIP website at www.cilip.org.uk/practice/employment.html. Other CILIP briefings on equal opportunities issues are also available at www.cilip.org.uk/practice/equalopps.html.

How to apply for a post

The basic rules in applying for a new post are extremely simple:

- Always read the details carefully.
- Submit your application in the way requested by the advertisement.

You can ask for further details or information if you wish at this stage.

Sometimes the organization's website will give the answer to your question(s). Increasingly adverts are carrying named individuals with whom you can have an informal chat. This is useful from both sides – it gives you an idea of whether you wish to progress with the application and also some idea of the detail of the work involved, which will not be revealed in an interview. From the organization's point of view it will save time and expense if the candidate decides after this informal chat that they do not wish to progress with the application.

If the advertisement tells you there is an application form, then obtain one quickly and complete it – you are likely to fall at the first hurdle if you simply submit your CV (there is more about CVs later in this chapter). Equal opportunities legislation encourages employers to gather information from applicants in a standard format.

Letters of application

Similarly, if you are asked to submit a letter of application, this should be more than just a covering note stating the obvious fact that it encloses a CV. The letter must contain a statement of your reasons for wanting the post, and some idea of your aspirations and plans for the position. It is unlikely that use of landscape letter layout will enhance your prospects.

Matching the employer's requirements

The clues to matching the employer's requirements are generally there in the advertisement, and in the application form too, if there is one. You will be asked for a range of information, and that can suggest the points that the interviewers are looking for in making their first selection of candidates to call to interview. In Chapter 1, we gave more detail about the kind of requirements that employers state they need in their advertisements (and warn against those who let you guess!) This chapter is about the ways to make your application, so you will need to refer to the Chapter 1 if you want to know more about the skills being asked for, rather than knowing how to write your application in reply to what the employer is asking for.

Application forms

Many jobs attract hundreds of candidates, and as a result application forms frequently specify the format and order in which information should be presented. Selectors expect to find information in that order on the application forms they receive and will not look kindly on your application if it does not comply with their format. Increasingly frequently, the form has been designed to be scanned (by a person or even a machine) so sending your details in a different format will rule you out in less than ten seconds. Your application may well lack information on a point that the employer considers important and it is more likely to be rejected as a result. It follows that you have only a short space of time in which to make an impression.

Fill in the form with relevant detail, not waffle, to show how your experience matches the requirements of the post. Your curriculum vitae (see next section) will tell the chronological story; you need to ensure that the rest of the documents show how the experience there makes you the best person for the job. If you do not match the specification exactly, but this is your dream job, you will have to make sure that you keep the selector's attention beyond the point when he or she discovers that you lack one or more of the skills the employer wanted; but be modest enough not to come across as pushy or arrogant. The employer might not have realised that a quality you possess was essential until your application pointed this out. You do not want to ruin the moment through arrogance!

Your CV

Even with an application form, you may be asked for your curriculum vitae (or CV, or resumé). This is a document that provides information about yourself, and most people are probably familiar with the basic concept. But a CV can be much more than this if you make it so. It is your opportunity to market yourself to your new employer, so make sure that you do!

Traditional CVs were a simple list of jobs held and the dates when you worked there. Most employers ask for such CVs to be presented in reverse chronological order of post. This allows them to see the current or most recent job first and to read further if they wish. But it does not allow you to present yourself in the best light to the selector. You need the opportunity to show how your skills and experience match the demands of the job.

Some candidates therefore adopt what is known as a functional layout. This concentrates on giving information about the type of work that has been done, rather than the times at which it was done. This approach allows the candidate to group types of work together to show how he or she matches the requirements of the post being offered (Figure 4.1).

Budgeting and management skills
Full responsibility to board of directors for library, managed budget of £xx,000 a year (Widget Industries Ltd)

Staff management
Managed three staff (Widget Industries Ltd), managed one customer services assistant and one filing clerk (Worm Castings Ltd)

Professional skills
Online searching and marketing (Widget Industries Ltd), providing information to intranet service and SDI alerting service (Worm Castings Ltd)

Fig. 4.1 *Functional layout*

It is an approach that has some drawbacks, quite apart from the obvious one that an employer will not welcome an application if it is deliberately couched in a different way from the one requested. A functional CV:

- allows the candidate to describe the function rather than the title of the post . . . but that could be done in inflated, overblown language (what is the difference between 'customer service representative' and 'counter assistant'?)
- allows the candidate to group together similar jobs related to the post on offer . . . but that could disguise how long (or short) a time was spent in those jobs
- allows the candidate to show the range of work he or she has covered, and the development of skills . . . and also allows unaccounted time to disappear (don't be coy – if you took six months off visiting India, say so).

The result of this problem is that some candidates present a 'combined approach' CV – that is, they give a functional analysis, which demonstrates that they have a strong claim on the job on offer, and then add a bare-bones chronological section.

Rather than just listing jobs, it is helpful to indicate major achievements in each post you held. Increasingly you will be asked specifically to list such achievements. An emerging approach is for the candidate to list the competences that he or she possesses and to use the job and training record to demonstrate these claims (see Figure 4.2). A claim to hold project management skills might be illustrated by a list of projects that the candidate has managed, or the ability to analyse computer software by details of work on a helpdesk.

A final point – do not rely on a list of what duties you have performed. Where possible include details of what you achieved, such as an increase in information provided or customers trained to obtain information successfully for themselves.

Anne Applicant
Library Manager, Widget Industries Ltd, Borchester, 2001–date
Library Customer Services Manager, Worm Castings Ltd, Birmingham,
1996–2001

Budgeting and management skills
Currently I have full responsibility to the board of directors for budgeting in the library, and manage a budget of £xx,000 a year.

Library automation project board manager (1997–98) – new system installed on time and below budget

Completed OU module in financial management (1996)

Staff management
Manage three staff (Widget Industries Ltd), managed one customer services assistant and one filing clerk (Worm Castings Ltd)

Library Association (now CILIP) course, Managing Difficult Colleagues (1999)

Professional skills
Online searching and marketing (Widget Industries Ltd), providing information to intranet service and SDI alerting service (Worm Castings Ltd)

Trained Dialog Information Services user (1998, attended update meetings 1999, 2001, 2002)

CILIP (formerly Library Association) course, Marketing your Library Service, 1998

Best Information Services course, Information for your Intranet, 1997

Fig. 4.2 *Demonstrating competencies*

Editing your CV for the post

You will probably need to fine-tune your CV to the post in question, if only to emphasize the skills you have to offer. If your technical skills include a knowledge of Unix and that is what the job needs, you need only refer briefly to your skills in other systems. If the employer wants to know if you can maintain the Unix web server as part of the job, he or she probably does not want to wade through your Windows NT management course certificates. Given the short time that the initial selector will spend looking at your application, if your relevant skills are not clearly visible in the first minute of reading, you can forget the new job.

If you are asked to complete an application form then do not submit just your CV instead. If you are asked to submit a letter of application in your own handwriting, it is not sensible to send only a printed document of application. And make sure that that you provide the required number of referees.

Answer the questions honestly and be sure not to omit details that might prove troublesome at interview. Many people leave gaps in their employment record where they may have been out of work or have decided to take an extended holiday. Interviewers examine the information that each candidate supplies, and are perfectly capable of identifying unexplained gaps in candidates' details. (We mentioned above the problems of hiding this in a functional CV.)

If you were looking for work for several months, then include this information in your application. At worst it can provide you with something to discuss with the interviewer. (Keep a copy of what you put on the application form and take it with you to the interview.) Many interviewers are familiar with talking to candidates who have been looking for work, and will value your honesty rather than your deceit in concealing what is nowadays a common situation.

Be sure to give full details where requested on the form. Employers are now obliged to ask a number of questions relating to nationality and citizenship, and some of these may seem unnecessary or peculiar. Bear in mind that these application forms are designed for use by a wide range of potential applicants and do not jeopardize your own application by omitting details that you think must be blindingly obvious, or skipping those that you think are impertinent questions.

By the same token, be scrupulously honest if you are claiming guaranteed interviews, for example under the Disability Discrimination Act. Not only is it despicable to claim an interview by pretending to be disabled; it is also illegal, and you will be found out at some time between applying for a job and the point where you would have been appointed. If the Act does apply to you, make sure you get what is yours by right.

If you are in a post that involves 'having substantial access to children or to vulnerable adults' – in the public library and school library sectors, for example – a further declaration will be required to ensure that you do not have any convictions or bindovers that could make you an unsuitable candidate.

Some forms ask for your full educational history, others ask for your secondary or even your post secondary education details only. You may also be asked to provide this information, like your employment history, in a particular chronological order. Make sure that you comply with the request. If all the other candidates have provided their history in reverse chronological order, and yours is in chronological order, your form will be at a disadvantage. If you are asked for schools and colleges attended since age 14 or 16, do not include your primary school!

Awkward details

One of the most difficult sections of an application form to complete is one asking for your reason for leaving previous positions. In completing this section, you should provide information that does not raise doubts in the interviewer's mind, so do not denigrate your previous employers or colleagues. Remember that many interviewers will begin looking at candidates with an eye to their future career, and will be seeking employees who will not go on to speak badly of their company or colleagues to some future potential employer.

Be particularly careful when describing the situation where you left a job for something better. Your potential employer will be wondering whether you will leave the new company, too, should something more attractive come along. You need to present a career move in a positive fashion to allay this kind of fear. Many candidates describe this situation by saying that their previous post gave no opportunity for promotion. This may indicate to an employer that the person has an inflated view of their own potential or promotability, and they may be wary of employing them as a result. It is better to say the post applied for appears to offer better long-term prospects.

Referees

You will almost certainly be asked to provide the names of referees when applying for professional posts, and often for paraprofessional positions too. These may well need to be people who have known you during your training and studies, especially if you are living in a new area while looking for work.

There are recent reports that employers are placing more emphasis on personal references as a way of distinguishing between a growing number of similarly qualified candidates. This emphasizes the importance of selecting a good referee – and of observing good manners. It is not only common courtesy to ask your referee's agreement before listing them, but it is also sound sense. People sometimes react badly to the discourtesy of finding that they are unexpectedly asked to provide a reference.

One of the authors remembers the reference provided by a distinguished elderly gentleman, his career in public and political service eventually rewarded by an appearance in the honours list, who found himself asked to act as a referee. He simply wrote, 'I do not think Richard will actually steal anything from you.'

Richard did not get the job.

Applying 'cold' for a job

It is often said that the best jobs are not advertised. They go by word of mouth, or head-hunters are employed to find candidates. This can happen with information service and library posts, although in some sectors such as the public services there are rules that preclude this kind of approach to filling many posts.

But what about the organization that you have set your heart on working for? Is it worth applying before a job has been advertised, or just in case – the library equivalent of cold calling? In many cases the answer is yes, although with some cautions. First, be ready for frequent rejection and letters telling you that any vacancies will be publicly advertised. Second, do not make yourself a nuisance. Try to discover whether unsolicited CVs are welcomed, or at least retained – and, if so, for how long. Renew your claim when your previous application is likely to be weeded. Third, make sure the CV you send is explicitly tailored to the organization; if you are bothering them about a vacancy that may not yet even exist, then our rules about tailoring your application apply even more strongly. If your CV is badly targeted it will get not any attention.

But you might expect to get some benefit from a 'cold' application. At the very best, you could get a job working where you aimed to work. Otherwise you will have your CV on their file, or know what their rules are on advertising vacancies. When there is next a job, they may even remember your name and invite you to interview. Only be sure that any benefit you gain is not outweighed by your colouring the opinion the organization might form of you. If the job for which you speculatively applied is advertised, apply again!

Spoilt for choice?

At some points in your career you will be holding more than one job offer. Which one will you go for?

The initial question must be: 'Which one do you truly want?' Money is not the only reason to pick a job, and as we saw above you may have to do considerable work to compare salaries between jobs. Which one comes nearest your ideal? Do you want to stop working weekends? Do you want to travel a shorter distance to work?

Other 'softer' factors are also important. Which looked the best place to work? Could you face working with or for your interviewer? Did you like the feel of one organization more than another? Did the library seem friendly, or busy, or welcoming . . . or dirty?

If you find that you did not get these questions quite right this time, think through the process. If there needs to be a next time for job seeking, learn from the experience!

In Appendices 1 and 2 (pages 167 and 172) we have provided a typical application form and a sample CV to help you.

Working in Europe case study revisited

In the first edition of this book, Case Study 4 looked at the skills that were required by employers in France, based on the wording of job vacancy advertisements in *ADBS Informations*, a French professional organization's monthly bulletin for its members. To see how the market had evolved, we studied a further set of about 50 advertisements that appeared in late 2002 and early 2003 for a range of professional posts in France. In the details below, the comparable 1998–9 figure appears in parentheses.

The market for first professional posts appeared weaker than in our first survey covering 1998–9. Language skills were again important, with English mandatory for just under 50% (62%) of the posts (and in the new sample two of the advertisements were in English). Other language skills were also asked for, German specifically.

As before, personal attributes were very important, sometimes being specified even though there was no statement of the professional skills required. Qualities most requested were:

- sector specific knowledge 44% (27%)
- team-working ability 36% (34%)
- accuracy 36% (21%)
- organizational skills 30% (21%)
- interpersonal skills 22% (14%).

Organizational skills were requested much more often than in earlier adver-tisements. Self-starter qualities (20%) and customer focus (18%) also gained in importance for employers in the more recent advertisements. Some of the qualities that are strange to British job seekers again appeared, such as intellectual curiosity, which was mentioned by 10% of advertisers. The ability to work under pressure was not mentioned at all (5% in 1998–9) – perhaps a reflection of the introduction of a statutory 35-hour week in France since our last survey.

The number of advertisements specifying the number of years of fur-ther education of the candidate to be supplied rose to 46% (34%); there was a requirement for a Master's in two more senior posts. Previous expe-rience was asked for in 50% (50%) of cases, with the sector of experience now being specified in 20% of the total sample; 12% (27%) of the sam-ple asked for at least two years' experience (so it seems that more relevant experience is being sought rather than simply the length of that experi-ence).

The software requirements remained similar, with 24% of advertise-ments asking either for general office software skills or for Microsoft products by name. However, 13% required mandatory knowledge of one (or in two cases both) of two information retrieval programs not mar-keted in the UK, putting these posts out of reach of many potential candidates. Communication skills remain a rare requirement, but edito-rial skills seemed to be in vogue: 12% of the posts asked for them, with some also asking for perfect spelling.

Summary

After reading this chapter you should know:

- how to apply for posts that interest you
- that research pays dividends
- what to include and what not to include in job applications
- that honesty is essential in applying for another job
- about the role of referees
- what to consider when choosing between two offers.

5

Next steps in your career, including promotion plans

In this chapter we consider:

- getting promoted and developing a job promotion plan
- going for another job in your own organization
- going for promotion in your own organization
- going for a similar or better job somewhere else
- changing sectors
- working from home.

Getting promoted and developing a job promotion plan

Most people want to be promoted and see their careers develop, but we accept and have known people who, for their own reasons, just want to stand still in their own particular jobs.

Different organizations promote people in different ways. Some promotions are made through merit, but most, if they are publicly funded, have to be through the competition route. Sometimes the process may be through an examination process that may include one or more of the following tests – written test, oral interview or performance test.

In theory you actually start preparing for your promotion the day you start working at your current job. If you wait until the promotion opportunity is announced, you're too late. In your interview for your current job you should have been told what the job opportunities are for career development. If you were not told, then you should certainly ask at interview what the long-term prospects are. So, as soon as you are in post, check with your supervisor or the personnel department in your organization to identify your promotional opportunities. Ask for job descriptions or prior job announcements for the jobs that you might be promoted into, and review the job descriptions or prior job announcements to get an understanding of the skills and expertise needed. Then you can start to plan and train if necessary for those job promotions. Identify in these jobs the major duties and responsibilities, and the skills, knowledge and abilities that are needed to carry them out.

Develop a job promotion plan

Set a goal for each major duty or responsibility in the job descriptions. Promotional opportunities typically occur every two to four years. So set your goals with the intention of being ready to apply for promotion in two years.

Prioritize

If you are particularly strong in one major duty, then focus on the other duties that you may need to improve to be able to apply for the next job. Therefore if there is a major duty or responsibility that you will be tested on for the promotion, place a higher priority on that duty or responsibility than on others. Periodically evaluate your progress in being able to perform the tasks that will be required in the jobs that you are interested in being promoted to.

Watch and learn from others

Talk to people in the jobs that you might be promoted to. Find out what they did to succeed and what they would do differently. Discuss the mistakes they made, how they see the job evolving, and what steps you should take to get promotion. Become a 'people watcher' and see how they perform. Also analyse what they do and how senior management staff react to their performance. Most of all learn from their successes and failures. If there is someone in the organization who would be happy to act as your mentor then seize the opportunity and accept their offer. See Chapter 3 for a discussion of the role of mentoring in helping people develop their skills and career plans.

Network

The authors believe that networking has been a major contributory factor to the development of their careers. Through networking you are learning all the time; remember that not everything gets written down or put on websites. Networking will enable you to keep up to date with the latest professional developments and trends.

Learn on the job

Just like any other profession, information jobs need the most suitably qualified and experienced person to fill the job and that will be somebody who has relevant experience in a similar job.

Consider volunteering for more difficult and responsible assignments, particularly if those assignments are similar to those required in your promotional plans. Learn how to get the job done and get it done right the first time. Consistency and effective work performance are valued by all supervisors and line managers and of course will be added to your continuing appraisal and development portfolio. Do not be too single minded about this; even if the assignments are not directly related to your promotional opportunities, volunteer and build your management's trust and confidence in you. That trust and confidence will earn you more opportunities to be considered for other duties and jobs.

Blowing your own trumpet is sometimes alien to information workers' idea of being a true professional but learn how to manage other people's perception of you. When you do a good job, make sure that your efforts are noted and recognized. And learn how to be big enough to admit it if you make mistakes, and at the same time learn from your mistakes and also from your successes. Remember that wherever you work or whatever you do, you will make mistakes and learn from them.

Train, train and train again

Never think that you are too old to learn. Although experience on the job is essential, always look to see if there are formal training courses or development opportunities. These may include in-house classes and external courses such as those offered by external training organizations. Look for distance learning opportunities to build your skills, enlarge your knowledge and abilities. You know what learning methods suit you and what skills you already have, but you may need to ask colleagues and friends to help you review your work and career plans. In Chapter 2 we looked at the idea of building a portfolio career, where you need to consider the changing trends and opportunities in the job market. The development of appropriate skills is increasingly seen as a personal responsibility because many people are on short-term contracts, and employers – and future employers – expect their workers to come to them with appropriate levels of skills and expertise for the work they will carry out. Going on training courses paid for by employers is seen as a privilege. You may even be asked to share any new skills with other less privileged colleagues.

The TFPL Knowledge and Information Skills Toolkit

Consider looking at the TFPL Knowledge and Information Skills Toolkit (www.tfpl.com), which was launched in Spring 2003 to enable individuals working in information management and knowledge management environments to assess their current skills levels. It also enables you to compare your skills against a number of skills profiles developed for roles of differing scope and seniority. The Skills Toolkit also links you to development resources for skills that you wish to strengthen. It can be used for personal development planning and as a management tool for team or individual development. The Toolkit encourages the individual to discuss their self-assessment with a line manager or colleagues. It assists in the assessment of the skills required in specific roles, evaluation of current skills levels, identification of skills gaps and points the way to develop and improve skills. The assessment is represented graphically using a spidergram.

After using this Toolkit you will be in a very good position to decide what your priority training needs are to enable you to reach your promotion goals.

Paying for training and free courses

Take advantage of tuition reimbursement programmes that may be on offer. But if your employer cannot or does not want to pay for your learning, and you want to take up a course that might be expensive, consider asking your bank for a loan. It is your career that you are investing in!

Not all courses will cost you money – if you look there are websites that offer free courses to help you with your development. Here are a few we have found:

- Smartcertify at www.smartcertify.com – IT courses among selected courses and sample questions from exams
- Digital University at www.digitaledu.com –a free sampling of online courses; past offerings include PowerPoint, e-commerce, and Internet Security

- Introduction to Java at www.javaworld.com – a free internet-based online class from IBM
- Microsoft at www.microsoft.com/traincert – offers learning tools.

Improve your presentational skills

You may also wish to look at your presentational skills and see if these can be improved. As information services are developed you will probably find that you are more and more required to give presentations about the services offered. Likewise, when you are applying for promotion, you may find yourself being asked to give a presentation to the interviewers on a special topic relating to the work in hand or to explain what you have been doing. Learn how to make and deliver a PowerPoint presentation, use videos correctly and improve your communication skills. There are many useful books, videos and training courses available in this area. And the time spent on improving your presentational skills will come in useful as your career progresses.

Your promotion plan

To sum up:

- keep your promotion plan up to date – just as you keep your CV updated
- watch the job adverts and keep abreast of the skills and experience currently being demanded
- learn from others – colleagues, managers, suppliers, contractors, consultants – keep up your networking; remember that there is always something new in the world
- learn from your successes and mistakes
- take up opportunities to learn another job, even for a short period of time
- take up further training courses
- hone your presentational skills, and if necessary take further training to improve them

- record all your successes alongside your training courses in your continuing professional development log book.

Going for another job in your own organization

It will depend on circumstances whether you find yourself being moved from job to job within your organization. Larger employers will have a range of posts at most seniority levels within their organization and there should be some kind of planned management of staff development that will allow transfer between posts. This rotation will provide the opportunity to carry out a range of professional tasks within the information service and to develop a variety of skills.

In a small organization there is unlikely to be the flexibility to allow this. At best there may be a small number of posts at a similar level – usually the basic professional grade – where exchanges are possible. However, you may find that you have to persuade unwilling colleagues to take on work in which they have little interest, and that the real opportunities are therefore limited. Another problem is that in a small information service after you have done the other job the only possible change is returning to your original job. The possibilities are therefore limited, and so quite probably is the long-term potential of the employer unless you are going to be content to do similar jobs in rotation for several years.

One alternative if you like your employer is to look for postings or secondment to other areas of the organization where you can either use your information skills or acquire other knowledge that will increase your value to the information service on your return. Librarians' ability to navigate information sources often makes them suitable to work in advisory roles and in customer service areas, where their training in dealing with people is an additional bonus. The only limitation is the bounds of your imagination, as a range of policy and case-working roles might be suitable. Research work might also be possible, making good use of graduate subject-specialist knowledge and of information-seeking skills.

Reading our book *Becoming a Successful Intrapreneur* (Pantry and Griffiths, 1998) may give you some ideas for lateral moves that could benefit your career, or suggest some areas in which you might want to work to acquire knowledge to use in your later career development.

If you find yourself reaching a dead end in your current job, you have three realistic options if you wish to move on:

- Going for promotion in your own organization
- Going for a similar job with another employer
- Going for a better job with another employer.

We shall look at these in turn and then look at other work options further on in this chapter.

Going for promotion in your own organization

Promotion with your existing employer is an option that is probably governed by practices peculiar to the organization. In some cases you may simply be selected for a vacancy and informed of your promotion. In many organizations strictly controlled promotion boards are required, with advertisements placed through official channels and formal applications made for vacant posts. If you have any choice in deciding whether to apply for promotion, it would be useful to carry out the SWOT analysis described below (Figure 5.1). If you decide to go ahead, use the advice in Chapter 4 to help complete the application form.

If you are promoted within your current organization, the conditions of work, good or bad, will probably be the same as in your present job, although the higher grade may gain some additional privileges or perks in return for additional responsibilities and maybe additional work. The question of salary is likely to be out of your hands unless an open bidding system applies and you are therefore able to negotiate your new salary. On the other hand, you will have narrowed the prospects of there being further promotion opportunities for suitable job swaps at the same level, meaning that in your medium-term career plan you would need to be considering how to find your next job even while you are learning the new one.

Another problem in being promoted in the same organization is that you often finish up supervising people you previously worked with as colleagues and with whom you may have exchanged complaints about the management. Now you are expected to become one of those very people you criticized! In an internal promotion interview you are very likely to be asked a question about how you would handle this – especially if one of the other candidates is a colleague whom you would have to supervise in future. Everyone's answer is different but that answer needs to be convincing – you need to prove, preferably by giving examples from your own experience, that you can do it!

Going for a similar job with another employer

Particularly if you have been doing very basic level work with your present employer, you will be able to apply confidently for posts doing similar work elsewhere. The job listings that we considered in Chapter 3 will be your main source of advertisements, although you might be able to obtain news of vacant jobs on the library grapevine. The jobs that are increasingly advertised on the Mailbase mailing lists are likely to be of more interest to you when you have been working for some time than to the newly qualified librarian. Where the vacancy also appears in print, the mailing lists often have the advertisement first.

Before you apply for a new post, consider what you are looking for this time, now that you have some experience in employment. What were the good and bad features of your previous employer? Carry out a SWOT analysis (listing Strengths, Weaknesses, Opportunities and Threats) on your last post and see how they map on to the new post. The result could look something like Figure 5.1.

Strengths	Weaknesses
• Good training policy	• Lack of progression
• Good employee benefits	• Poor physical surroundings
• 20 days' leave a year	• Poor catering and a long way
• Investors in People status	from town
• Good after-work social life	
Opportunities	**Threats**
• Boss has six months to retirement and the post could be available	• Recession means funding is shaky and the library may be vulnerable
• Entitlement to ten training days each year	• IT section is making a stronger bid than library to run knowledge management
• Chances to travel to conferences and make yourself better known	

Fig. 5.1   *SWOT analysis*

By working through this process you will have a clearer picture of whether and why you really want to leave your present post. Carrying out the same process using what you know about the second post and the employer will allow you to focus even more clearly on what you hope to gain from your possible move, and whether the post on offer is the right one for you. You might in fact come to the conclusion that the right thing to do is to stay put until something better comes along.

Salary will clearly be a further influencing factor. It would be too mechanical and rigid to base your choice of post solely on allocating scores to each job and dividing the salary offered by that score, giving you a 'pounds per point' rating for the job. But it might be an interesting exercise that could give you a final clue if you are finding it difficult to decide between competing offers. Consider that if the best-paid job available looks boring and has no prospects, it is probably not the best job on offer.

Going for a better job with another employer

A better job with another employer brings together the risk factors from both the previous options. On the negative side, you would be going through the stresses of dealing with the more senior work and the change of organization at the same time. Even if you are familiar with the type of organization you are considering moving to, for example a council in the public sector, there can still be cultural and procedural differences between employers. You need to apply all of the techniques we have discussed to be certain that applying for the job in the new organization is a good career move, and that the organization itself is right for you. On the positive side, you will not have to manage former workmates, and there may be further opportunities with the new employer.

Demonstrating your value to a future employer

In all of these cases it would be important for you to be able to demonstrate to your employer, present or potential, what value you have and what skills and versatility you can call on in your work. The best way of demonstrating this is through maintaining your curriculum vitae – your CV – and presenting this in support of your application for a new post. We looked at some different approaches to compiling a CV in Chapter 4.

You should also keep an up-to-date statement relating to your experience that can be brought in to a suitable letter of application. In all but the smallest organizations you may be asked to make such a statement when applying for a post; even if it is not specifically requested, ask yourself whether it would be worthwhile including a suitable (short) supporting statement.

Referees

You should consider finding referees who can provide a statement of support for your application as any application form that you are asked to fill in when applying for a job with a new employer will probably ask for them. The application form will often specify the type of referees required so you will have to list current or previous employers, or your university or college. The correct practice when naming an employer is generally to name the organization rather than an individual, who will in any case probably have to pass the letter to a central personnel office where records are kept. Where you are naming someone you have worked with, make it clear when you are naming him or her in a personal capacity.

It is a common courtesy – far too often overlooked – to ask someone whom you want to act as a referee in a personal capacity if they are willing to take on this role before giving their name in your job application. Failing to do so risks the annoyance of your referee and consequently a less than flattering reference.

Be sure that your referees can speak between them for the range of your abilities. Academic and work referees will provide the detail of your previous experience and suitability for the post in question. Personal referees can comment on your character and personality, but remember that they may be able to say little of your true professional skills.

Many organizations will save themselves the cost of obtaining references for every candidate for a post; some will only call for the references of short-listed candidate or even their final nominee, but they will probably call for your references at some time before appointing you. (They will normally respect your request not to contact an existing employer until a firm offer is being made.) So ensure that as full a picture as possible will be given by the referees whom you choose, and that what they have to say will match what you have written on the application form. If you think you will need your referees more than once, sort all this out before you make any job applications.

It would do no harm to thank your referees after applying for a new job, whether or not you are successful, in case you need to ask them to act as referees again. And if they have helped you get a better job, let them share a little of your success for their contributions!

Finally, bear in mind that not only references have to be taken up if you are offered a new job. Depending on the type of work, other checks have to be made such as security checks for some areas of government, and checks with various registers for work with children and vulnerable adults. It can take several weeks to complete these; do not quit your current job until you are certain they have all been successfully completed!

Changing sector

One simple statement can be made on this question. Changing employment sectors in library and information work can be difficult, but it can also allow you to build on your existing skills and to offer an employer the benefit of your knowledge in another sector. To achieve this may well require your full range of marketing skills. You need to sell not only yourself and your abilities, but put a positive spin onto your desire to leave your current sector and start again in another kind of work.

Changing sector is easiest at the early stages of a career. Certainly in the first years there may be a positive benefit in doing so if you want to progress to more senior levels. Subject knowledge is often a key; so for example a law librarian could find work in any number of law firms, in the academic sector, or in government libraries, and so on. Health and medical libraries are another sector where the range of posts is widening as the skills of information professionals become better known and mobility between types of library appears relatively simple.

On the other hand, transferring to an academic library at more senior levels without a long and relevant career record is uncommon. In some sectors, notably central government, the methods of recruitment preclude external candidates taking vacant posts unless all internal avenues have been exhausted. Lack of experience in local government finance and management expertise would effectively prevent a candidate from transferring to the highest level posts in public libraries.

During local government reorganization, some posts have been designated as available only to people already working in the sector, so as to protect existing careers. Were such events to happen again, you could find as people did then that the choice of posts suitable for a career change of sector becomes limited.

The best advice would be to try different sectors at the early stages of a career if you are uncertain in which sector to work in the longer term. Go on visits organized by your professional body; organize work visits to your neighbours in other types of library. Then aim to develop the skills and knowledge (especially of financial and management procedures) that you need to reach the top of your chosen sector. You might also bear in mind that if you intend to go into consultancy at any point, knowledge of the range of library sectors will be useful.

Working from home

There are two possible reasons for working from home. First, that you are working on your employer's business in your home for reasons of your or your employer's convenience; second, that you are working independently on your own account. We shall be looking at reasons and opportunities for becoming a fully independent consultant in a later chapter. But what if you decide to work from home while still employed, perhaps because of family commitments, or to reduce commuting?

In these days of advanced communications and technologies there is often no reason why some part of your work cannot be carried out from your home. There are many advantages for employers and employees in staff working from home, for some of the time at least. Some of the benefits may be:

- ability to concentrate better on the work in hand
- fewer interruptions
- no travel time and consequently no daily exhaustion!
- having time to explore ideas and carry out research.

Although it is clearly difficult for someone in a traditional library environment to work from home when the reference collection is 40 km away, it is quite feasible for someone engaged on research or electronic current awareness to do the work from their own sitting room or study and send the results to the main organization by fax or e-mail. Knowledge-based working is being increasingly quoted as a growth area for homeworking, and the possibilities were described recently by one commentator as being 'endless'.

Among the disadvantages of homeworking are some that militate against doing LIS work from home:

- lack of social contact
- lack of access to files
- difficulty in talking to colleagues
- difficulty in meeting colleagues and other people.

Interestingly, most of these disadvantages relate to communication with people – colleagues, customers and social contacts – and modern communications make it far easier to make and maintain these contacts. So we suggest that if your work is mainly with electronic information sources that you access online, and your customers are remote (telephone, e-mail or fax contacts), then you could probably work successfully at home if you can provide a suitable working environment.

In this case you should think about whether you can provide a separate work area in a part of your home. It needs adequate or good furniture (you will not work well at a rickety second-hand desk) and you should preferably have a separate telephone line. Consider where you are going to put papers and documents. Your employer may insist on carrying out a health and safety audit of your home to ensure that the working area meets the required standards.

Many homeworkers find they work best by pretending to go to the office, sometimes by physically going out and coming back in, certainly by dressing in a business-like manner, and often by doing something concrete like closing a door on the rest of the home when beginning work.

Some final words: if you work at home make sure that you do not become the resident parcel collector for all your neighbours, think carefully if there is already a teleworker in your house – especially if you are the one who will make the coffee every time – and make sure you visit your base in the central workplace often enough to be remembered!

Summary

In this section we have looked at various options for moving on. You should have some ideas about these questions:

- Is it time for your next move?
- Do you want to stay with your present employer?
- What are the advantages and disadvantages of a new employer for jobs at the same level?
- And for more senior jobs?
- Could you work from home instead?

6

Your successful interview

In this chapter we are going to consider how to reach and prepare for interviews, the interview itself, and also look at two kinds of interview: the recruitment interview and the promotion interview.

You will discover:

- how people reach interview
- what interviewers are looking for
- what you can find out at the interview and what you should find out before
- what kinds of interview there are and what other tests you might face
- why appearance and behaviour matter at a selection interview
- what you should ask at interview (and what not to ask)
- what to think about if you are going for a promotion interview
- the dos and don'ts of recruitment interviews.

For many people interviews are the most stressful part of their career development. What are they going to ask me? What are they looking for? Will they try to catch me out? It may be some comfort to remember that interviews are stressful for many interviewers too!

Getting to the interview stage

In a moment we will describe some of the different forms of interviews and other selection procedures. But some general comments on behaviour are in order first.

The candidates for any kind of selection interview or test have been chosen from their presentation on paper, whether that is by application form, CV, or letter of application. They will have provided some standard information (age, education, qualifications, and so on) and a description of their career to date and perhaps their aspirations. They should have a sales pitch to sell themselves as the best candidate for the job, and now they have been invited to an interview. We looked at this process in detail in Chapter 4. There is now very substantial evidence that the selection process is becoming longer and more rigorous. Several factors are contributing to these trends and it is important that these are appreciated. There are greater expectations, so candidates need to be able to demonstrate clearly how flexible and adaptable they are; how they have the right drive, determination and experience; their creativity; and that they are able to cope with uncertainty better than the next candidate. If these seem to be very tall orders, then they are, but by being aware of these trends the candidate is on the way to a successful interview.

What interviewers are looking for

No interviewer wants to be the person who took on a square peg to fill a round hole in the organization. First and foremost, then, interviewers are looking for somebody who can meet their 'person specification' for the position and fit into the team and the organization at large. They have only a short time to make their choice, based on the interview, although you should have given them plenty of guidance in your application. They will be looking for someone who can communicate well with other people (especially the stranger conducting the interview), and in the case of information specialists they may well be looking for someone who can put across specialist and technical information in clear layperson terms. In a negative sort of way, interviewers are also looking for the awkward, ill-matched or difficult candidates in order to keep them out of the organization. Up to the interview, the candidates are simply names and data on sheets of paper. The interviews put faces to that information and allow the interviewers to select the person (or persons) whom they think will fit best into their organization, in terms of skills and of personality. Interviews give selectors only a short time to make their choice and give you only a short time to convey your message and your personality. Every second counts; so it will pay you to prepare well and think about how you are going to approach the interview to ensure you have your proper say.

Preparing for your interview

You cannot predict all the questions you will be asked in your interview, but you can make some intelligent guesses at the kinds of area likely to be covered. If you are being interviewed for a specialist post (such as a cataloguer or a research analyst) you could predict that questions will be asked relating to these areas. Your skill should be taken for granted, based on the application you have submitted, and technical skills like cataloguing are difficult to test in an interview. However, you could expect a practical test of some of these skills (for example, being asked to catalogue some items before or after your interview) and for example you are likely to be asked about the principles of analysis or current awareness (such as 'How would you go about choosing items for inclusion in a bulletin?').

Research your potential employers – and their sector, if appropriate. Find out what is in their last annual report and notice which areas of their business they have highlighted. Discover what other interests, business or recreational, their senior staff have. If they are listed in biographical directories, so much the easier. And what do their competitors think is important? Have your potential employers been in the news lately? If they are a large company or a public body, they almost certainly have been.

Even a small company may have made it to the local press, but at least find out what is important in their line of business and be ready to point to or comment on events in that sector.

What you can do to improve your chances in the interview

Before you go for interview consider the possible interaction that is likely to take place and decide if you are selling yourself, persuading or negotiating, imparting information or discussing a topic. You should go in for an interview with a positive attitude; you may be nervous, but endeavour to make an impression on the interviewers through judicious use of eye contact with the questioner, then scanning the others on the panel to reinforce your answers. Be aware of the body language of the interview board members: nods, glances and smiles.

Kinds of interview

An interview can take several forms, which will depend on the culture of the organization that you are applying to. You can expect that a public sector body is likely to be more formal about the conduct of an interview than a consultancy or a small business. But even this is not a hard and fast rule as agencies and other areas of the public sector adopt a more free-wheeling approach; they see this as being more commercially minded than holding a formal board. Small organizations may make their procedures more formal in order to ensure that they do not discriminate against any of the candidates.

Unstructured interviews

Unstructured interviews are loosely organized; the discussion is often far-ranging, with the focus shifting on those issues that may be of greatest interest to the interviewer, or those that may give some indication of future job performance – perhaps not the most satisfactory format for evaluating candidates.

Structured interviews

Structured interviews are very common and involve being interviewed by a panel of two or more people. In a structured interview candidates may be asked to clarify points or examples they have made in their application form. Therefore it is crucially important that you know and remember all the information that you submitted. We suggested in Chapter 4 that you keep a copy of your application form and take it to the interview to avoid being surprised by a detail you have forgotten. Members of the interview panel will ask for examples of your core skills and experience. The interviewers will ask you to provide specific and detailed examples when answering questions of past or current experiences. You may find that some attention will centre around how much additional training or development you may need.

The skills areas of your application form will be thoroughly explored but not necessarily in the same order as appeared in the application form. You may also be asked to provide other examples than those submitted, so it is advisable to have several specific examples in mind to illustrate the skills listed in the job specification. In a structured interview the questions are extremely specific so reply with the same structure to your answers. Listen carefully as there is a set time for each question and response: even if you appear to have time for rambling answers, you are eating into the total time allowed by the interviewers' schedule and you will end up getting fewer questions to discuss than other candidates. Look for signs of interest as well as indifference through eye contact and body language.

There are likely to be some common features in all interviews. One or more people will talk to you for something between 20 minutes and an hour, depending on the post being offered. Questions will be asked of you, often with little relationship to each other, so be prepared to switch topics quickly. After the questions, you should be given an opportunity either to give any further details about yourself, or to ask questions about the job. A skilled interviewer will ensure that the applicant does 70% of the talking. The interviewers will record their impressions once you have left the room. At the end of the session they will try to put the candidates whom they have seen into an order of preference, and make their recommendation for the person to be appointed.

Two-part interviews

In an organization that employs a specialist recruiter, usually a personnel manager, the interview may be in two parts. The first part should be devoted to an exchange of information about your CV and what the organization or company has to offer. The second part may be with the manager who has the vacancy and is obviously the one to impress with your LIS skills and previous experience.

For some jobs this process may run over several days or even weeks and the task of picking a winner or winners can be quite problematic in those circumstances. But however frustrating it is to the candidate, it is also frustrating and wasteful to the employer as many good candidates will tire of waiting and take other offers. If you find yourself in this position, do tell the prospective employer that you want to withdraw from the competition. It may make their task easier, and it will ensure that should you apply to them for a post again you will not be remembered for your discourtesy. Conversely, many employers do treat candidates with scant consideration, but unfortunately it is the employers who have the work to offer.

Panel interviews

Especially in the public sector, you may encounter three or even more interviewers. The technique you will have to use is quite different from being in a one-to-one discussion; but it has the balancing compensation that you will not be subject to the whim of a single interviewer who you may fail to get on with, or who may know nothing about information and library work. In a panel interview, a chairman (who may or may not be a specialist) will open the discussion, probably by asking some general questions about your career, or your interests and outside activities. Other panel members will then ask questions on professional issues, or on topical matters connected with the employer's business, or indeed related political and social issues.

Details of the interview

Your application form will have shown your expertise and skills, but your interviewer(s) are looking for your potential to do the job on offer. That is why they want to interview you. During the interview you must fill the gaps that the application form by nature does not cover, relating stories about your skills and past experiences and relating them to the job you are applying for.

Talk about goals and where you want to go in the future. Discuss your previous leadership successes, going over projects. Talk about the responsibilities you have taken and how you directed or assisted the outcome.

When talking about your job experience do not just list your previous employers. Talk about your achievements and amplify them – for example:

- I have experience in . . .
- I led a team of x number of people, some of whom needed training . . .
- These are the skills or insights I have gained as a result . . . and I can see them being of benefit in the job on offer.
- I have planned and managed a budget of £x – I understand what is involved in the planning, delivering and successful completion of a project . . . (show precise understanding of what is involved in the job).
- I know what would be expected in carrying out . . .

- Based on my experience/education and understanding of this work I can do . . .

As far as vocabulary is concerned, use empowering verbs – I can, I will, I believe, I know – but try not to be too bombastic.

Honesty counts. If you either do not understand or cannot answer the question say 'I don't know.' It will be apparent anyway. A willingness to acknowledge what you need to learn or what skills you wish to develop is better than bluffing. And if you bluff the interviewers may ask a further connected question that will stump you completely. A good interviewer will explain, or remind you of, enough detail to elicit the information they were seeking through the question, but some interviewers will simply change the subject, giving you no clue what they were seeking to find. This is poor practice, but all you can do is move on with them and not be distracted by this rebuff.

Be aware that recruitment agencies may interview you first on behalf of their client. You may have asked the same agencies to put you on their list of specialists, so they may well have interviewed you already before they added you to their list and will know quite a bit about you already. They will also have advised you on whether your skills meet the demands of the client. They can be helpful in telling you where your skills and expertise may need upgrading and will even help you achieve these standards.

Other tests

Employers seem to be becoming increasingly fond of additional activities around the interview. In some cases, candidates spend a whole day at the employer's premises, and are scheduled to undergo a number of tests and visits, of which the formal interview is only part. Although this is nerve-racking for many people, it has the compensation of giving a far more rounded view of candidates than a straight half-hour interview.

Giving a presentation

You may be asked to make a presentation on a topic of interest to your potential employer. This can take the form of a five- or ten-minute talk on a subject that has been notified to you a few days before your interview. You may be given an overhead projector or other audiovisual equipment to use during the presentation. Ensure that you are able to use the equipment before you start. It is very distracting for your audience if you are constantly hunting for switches or trying to put your slides in order. Keep your presentation to the point and remember your audience's interests.

Number your slides, make yourself a script, and follow it rather than trying to read from the slides. Make use of the features of PowerPoint or your chosen presentation software to print out a script with copies of the slides (the Notes page facility), even if you have to make transparencies rather than using a computer projector. However, do not be tempted to use all the bells and whistles if you are running the show from a computer – the middle of the interview is the wrong place to find out that the machine gun sound effect is totally inappropriate, as is building the slide letter by letter from all sides. Make notes on your paper copy telling you when to change slides. Once you have turned on the overhead projector, leave it switched on. The panel want to hear what your views are on the topic, not to know whether or not you can operate a switch. If the projector bulb burns out, that is a problem for someone else.

Psychometric tests

Some employers now use psychometric testing as a means of assessing candidates. You will be given either a sheet of questions with multiple choice answers, or perhaps a small machine like a calculator into which you enter your choices. After about 20 minutes, the paper is taken away and marks allocated by trained assessors. There are no right or wrong answers to these tests, which is why some people think they have very limited value. If you are lucky, you will get a session with a qualified occupational psychologist who will give you feedback before reporting the results to the employer.

There are reports that some employers are starting to use more aggressive forms of these tests such as a test called the Hogan Development Survey, which aims to identify poor behaviour when the candidate is under stress. Others use risk assessment methods alongside psychometric testing. Whatever your view, you will be very unfortunate if the selection of the successful candidate is based on the results of these tests alone. If they are used, it should be only to provide a better picture of the interviewees to complement selection interviews. Check the reading list for some websites to explore on psychometric testing techniques.

IQ and EI tests

An area that is starting to gain employers' attention is emotional intelligence (EI). Intelligence quotient (IQ) has been used as a recruitment tool for decades. Many major employers now use assessment centres to select new trainees, and invariably include aptitude tests as part of the procedure. There are several reasons these tests are so popular:

- They are generally considered to be objective and hence gender and race neutral.
- All candidates have the same questions and the same conditions and time in which to answer them.
- They are also believed to show candidates' ability to understand and interpret data – in other words, the skills they need to show in their jobs.
- Aptitude tests are also said to be a good indicator of future job performance.

However, critics claim that IQ tests measure only what IQ tests measure – that is, they show candidates' ability to answer the type of question used in IQ tests. They also say that IQ does not have a bearing on how people will perform in the practical, day-to-day elements of their work.

Today increasing numbers of employers, especially in the US, are starting to look instead, or as well, at emotional intelligence. The UK Chartered Institute of Personnel and Development has been informing its members about EI for some time now. Candidates are being judged by a new yardstick: not just by how smart they are, or by their training and expertise, but also by how well they handle themselves and others.

Daniel Goleman, author of *Working with Emotional Intelligence* (2000), describes emotional intelligence as 'the capacity for recognizing our own feelings and those of others, for motivating ourselves, and for managing emotions well in ourselves and in our relationships'. Thus EI is vital to understanding yourself and others.

In employment terms, this makes EI important in your ability to work with colleagues, bosses and subordinates, helping you to understand what is motivating them and therefore how to manage situations better. EI tests are based not on problem-solving but on how you react to given scenarios.

Supporters say that this makes it far more powerful than IQ in career development, as people with a high EI are able to handle people and situations skilfully and as a result progress further in their company. It is sometimes said that while IQ can get you a job, EI will get you promoted.

The principles of EI have been used in recruitment for some time, through the range of personality questionnaires that are used by many employers. These are not tests but questionnaires designed to reveal your thinking and work styles and thus show recruiters how you react in different situations. From this information they can draw conclusions about how well you will work with colleagues and in teams, fit into the company culture, and so on. This is important: you might be great at what you do, but if you don't work well in a team, and the potential employer has a team-oriented ethos, then the chances are they won't give you the job.

Watch your appearance

It is trite but very true that you only get one chance to make a first impression. If yours is awkward you will start your interview with a disadvantage. Start by being sure that your style of dress is appropriate. If your prospective employer runs a formal organization, turning up in casual clothes is a very bad idea. (Jeans are probably a bad idea in most interviews for library and information work anyway.) If the employer is in a more informal sector, then a more relaxed style is in order. However, even in some traditionally unstuffy organizations, a surprisingly smart style is expected, especially among professional groups. One good way of finding out the form is to ensure that you see the library before the day of the interview, and use the opportunity to observe the dress code of the organization.

Accessories rather than clothes often provide the chance to make a statement of individuality; perhaps consider wearing a modern tie or scarf to lighten a plainer suit. Even here it is easy to make an error. One survey (Cartoon, 1999) reported that men who wear ties decorated with cartoon characters come across as immature and having bad taste rather than a wacky sense of humour. In the same survey a large majority of managers thought that the choice of tie was an important factor in making first impressions and that unsuitable appearance at work lessened chances of promotion. Other surveys have linked colour with the messages conveyed to interviewers; neutral colours are the safest choice for clothing at interview.

If you want to bring any paperwork with you carry it in a smart file or briefcase, and please NOT in a plastic shopping bag. It might be as well to sort the documents within the file. Effective plastic files and dividers cost no more than a couple of pounds and can be highly effective. Remember you are trying to get a post as an information professional!

Jewellery should be carefully considered, and should complement rather than dominate your appearance. Some interviewers are still frightened by rings worn other than on fingers, or visibly pierced body parts other than earlobes. You can resume wearing such decorations once the job is yours, but on a first meeting you should restrict them to the minimum you feel to be true to yourself and your wish for employment. The same comment goes for hair worn in primary colours rather than the more traditional shades, or outside the accepted norms of length for either gender.

One of the many tip sheets for interviews suggests carrying an emergency kit in that smart briefcase, containing the following: moist tissues and facial tissues, a trial-size mouthwash, cologne, a nail file, brush or comb, personal business cards, two extra copies of your CV, a blank notepad together with a reliable pen (preferably one without an advertising slogan on it), Post-it notes, paper clips and sticky tape. (The tape doubles up for removing fluff from dark clothes.) Female candidates are recommended to add spare hosiery if wearing a skirt.

Getting to the interview

You will probably be shown to your interview by an escort – a messenger or a member of staff. If a member of staff has been allocated to shepherd interviewees there may be the chance to overhear a little of what is of interest or concern that day, or for a few words with the 'minder'. The staff member may well be asked afterwards for any impressions of candidates, so it can do no harm and quite probably some good to be friendly and interested.

Make sure you get to the interview in good time so that everybody you meet in the organization sees you at your best. Check where the nearest public transport or car park is, and be prepared for a traffic jam or for the tube in London to be closed when you calculate your travelling time. Other major cities in the UK and around the world suffer the same traffic congestion problems, so always allow yourself extra time. If you are travelling any distance, check travel information pages on teletext or on the world wide web before setting off, to identify any potential delays. Use any spare time when you arrive at your place of interview to freshen up (using the content of your emergency kit) and be ready for the interview with a couple of deep breaths. Most organizations will nowadays hope that you had a cigarette (if you needed one) somewhere other than on their front step before you came in. Read anything that looks relevant in the waiting room but don't overload your memory. The contents of the magazine table will give another clue to the organization: do they put the latest current affairs and business sector magazines in the room, or the library's year-old discards?

Starting the interview

Actions can speak louder than words and, particularly in interviews, it pays to be aware of body language and what it says about you. According to the experts, people form 90% of their opinion about a person within the first 90 seconds of meeting them, so ensure that you get your entrance right. Making a point of going into the interview room with confidence and on entering the interview room take time to settle. This is the time when nervous candidates fall over furniture, or spill water jugs as they sit down (if you take your own bottle of mineral water, break the seal and then close the top firmly again before you go in). Approach the candidate's chair calmly, and use the time for the social pleasantries to assess your surroundings. In the time it takes the chairperson or interviewer to introduce the people in the room, you can check whether there is some water within reach, whether the chair is at a comfortable height (do not try to adjust it but note whether you are likely to have to control your fidgeting as a result), or whether you have encountered any of the interviewers before.

The interview starts as soon as the candidate walks into the room. The seating arrangements do not always follow the traditional formal boardroom environment; nowadays you may equally expect a couch 'chat'.

Interviewers will be looking for people who impress quickly as good team players with the ability to communicate easily and effectively. Establish comfortable eye contact: interviewers are frightened by people who clamp on an unrelenting stare, and are annoyed by candidates who look at the carpet, the light fittings and the furniture but not at the people they are talking to. An easy style (as close to a chat with another staff member as you can muster in the circumstances) allows you to look occasionally not only at the interviewer but also at any other panellists, ensuring that you spot any signs of puzzlement or boredom on their part – suggesting you need to explain more, or stick closer to the point.

So look to your body language. Use it to show interest and establish rapport with your interviewers. Curb your tendency to fiddle if that is what you do when nervous; leave your jewellery alone and keep your fingers away from your face. Use your hands to adopt listening postures, and show interest in what is being said as well as what is being asked. Lean slightly towards your interviewers without flopping onto the desk – a posture almost as bad as sliding back into the chair and collapsing slowly downwards as the interview progresses! If you are uncomfortable with your posture and the messages it conveys, look at a book on body language – but be sure to do it some time before your interview so you are not self-conscious about it on the big day. Be professional throughout and act maturely – curb any tendency to use childish gestures or behaviour. Think of the effect you are having on the interviewers and their perception of you as a professional person and potential colleague.

How to use body language in an interview

Watch the body language of the interviewer and copy if appropriate. The following tips should be noted:

- *Give a firm handshake* – A recruiter's first impression of you is often formed when you shake hands. A firm handshake will give the right impression. But not too firm – that can seem arrogant or too challenging.
- *Sit comfortably* – Ensure that you are not facing bright sunshine as this

will detract from your concentration. (The interviewers should have sorted the position of chairs and tables.) Also ensure that you can see all the interviewers from where you are sitting and sit up straight. Do not sit with your legs crossed as this may cause you to fidget over the period of the interview.

- *Lean forward* – Leaning forward when the interviewer does or occasionally paraphrasing what he or she has just said can give a positive message. This suggests that you have an intense interest in what the interviewer is saying.
- *Tilt your head to the side* – A head held straight up signals a neutral attitude to what you're saying. A head tilted to the side means you've caught your interviewer's interest. A head held downwards is negative and judgemental.
- *Watch your hands* – No matter how nervous you are, try to avoid hand-to-face gestures such as touching your nose or rubbing your eye.

During your interview

The chairperson's introduction should allow you to relax into the interview (as far as that is possible!). You may be asked a difficult question early on, so do not relax too much. It might be a trick question, although that is really a case of bad interviewing technique. However, if you really want to work for an organization that employs this person, you will have to think on your feet and regard it as a sign of what is to come.

Sadly, many generalists in the chair of an information specialist board ask even the most senior candidates why they wanted to be librarians (rarely expressed, we find, in terms of why they chose the profession or the career). The best answer is to grin and bear this, perhaps prefacing the reply with an appropriate comment to the effect that your decision was made a long time ago and the profession has developed enormously since that time. But if there is a question that is truly intrusive about your private or personal life, refuse firmly but politely to answer it.

You are likely to be asked early on why you want to work for this employer. This should not be a difficult question and you should prepare an honest answer in advance. You should have done some research about the employer as part of your preparations, so you should have much of the information to hand. Emphasize the positive qualities of your potential new employer and not the negative features of your current work. Focus on work issues rather than people problems. And never make slighting comments about your current employer – the interviewer will be thinking about what you might say about their organization in future.

After the 'warm-up' questions, usually covering previous career history and your qualifications, there will be a discussion that will cover things like your knowledge of professional issues of general interest and those that particularly affect the interviewer. You can expect a test of your knowledge and understanding of what the organization does, probably including questions designed to find out if you share its values. There will also be questions designed to see how you manage and how you deal with everyday work situations. Always try to talk positively, in terms of what you have done, rather than give theoretical answers that start 'First of all I would . . . ' and resemble the instructions for building a Blue Peter model.

Be prepared for members of the board to write things down, whether or not you are speaking to them at the time. The chairperson or single interviewer should be taking notes to ensure that all candidates have been given the same chance, and any other interviewers should be noting down comments on professional and other specialist matters. You should perhaps be more alarmed if nobody writes anything down during the entire interview.

Discussion of professional issues may prove difficult when there is only one specialist on a panel of generalists. This is particularly awkward when you are going in on the first morning of an interview session, because the lay people (who will often include the chairperson) will not have had the time to start learning from candidates' answers. But by the second afternoon you could expect questions based on the layman's knowledge taken from the answers of previous candidates, so there may then be misconceptions to correct with the gentlest of firm hands that you can manage!

Many candidates fail to impress because they have become rather wooden. They answer without either engaging the interest or the attention of the interviewer, and fail to offer 'hooks' onto which further discussion can be hung. Closed answers, particularly those that consist of a simple 'yes' or 'no' with a minimum of extra content, offer no chance for the interview to become a dialogue and a discussion rather than an interrogation. Try to use open answers that invite further questions to which you already have the answers ready.

Interviewers despair when candidates use up all the prepared topics in the first five minutes. If you give short, unconsidered and undeveloped answers you may well find that after the first ten minutes the questioning becomes patchy and somewhat despairing. On the other hand, if you can achieve rapport with your interviewers in the available time, and make them feel they are learning from you, you are halfway home and dry. (The other half, of course, requires you to know what you are talking about.)

Promotion interviews

If you are going for a promotion interview in your current organization, remember that there are a number of people who can influence the result of whether or not you will be promoted. The reason that you have been invited for interview is that you have already impressed your management that you are good enough for the job, but they still want to interview formally, perhaps alongside candidates from outside the organization. The interview panel may include your line manager and other interviewers called in for their expertise and impartiality.

Previously, in appraisal, you will have decided for yourself if you are the right material for promotion and will have answered the following questions:

- Are you good enough for promotion? If you are honestly able to say yes to this question, then you are more than halfway to being promoted.
- Do you understand where your starting position is, where you need to get to, what you need to demonstrate, what you will be judged against, including competition from outside?
- Do you understand why your employers have written the job description with their 'perfect' candidate in mind?

Your line manager will have endorsed your application, so that should give you added confidence when you go for interview. Being promoted internally is a gamble on the part of a number of people including yourself, your current line manager and the new line manager. Your current line manager is putting his or her reputation on the line for you. So you need to sell yourself to the new manager.

The majority of organizations now measure employee performance. A common system used is that of annual appraisals, where your performance is reviewed. This will also be taken into account together with your application for the new job. You need to show what you have achieved for the organization and what you have learned over the past year or so, including giving details of any new qualifications, or examinations or courses you are currently taking. Also emphasize any new projects and whether or not they have been successful. It is suggested that you try and think two levels higher than the job you are going for – this will give the management an appreciation that you know where your career ladder is pointing.

Career ladder promotion?

A career ladder is the normal grade progression through which employees advance to reach the full-performance level (top grade of the career ladder) of a particular occupation, when the employee meets all requirements. A career ladder consists of grades ranging from the lowest level at which an employee can be hired to the highest level grade, also known as the full performance level.

In most organizations to advance to the next level in a career ladder, an employee must:

- meet qualification requirements
- meet time-in-grade requirements
- be recommended by his or her supervisor for promotion (remember that career ladder promotions are not guaranteed).

Line managers should ensure that employees are provided with increasingly difficult assignments and training, and these in turn prepare you for the next higher grade.

The promotion interview itself

At a promotion interview you will have the advantage of knowing the organization and most of the people interviewing you, but this in itself can be a problem because your attitudes, experience and performances are well known. Prepare for and answer the questions posed to you as if you are meeting these people for the first time.

If you have ever been passed over for a promotion that you thought you deserved, you will have re-evaluated your situation to understand why this happened, and you should have addressed some of the points raised in the feedback to you. Do bring this up at your next promotion interview.

You will have let it be known that you are interested in moving up the promotion ladder. Even if you are the ideal candidate for the job, if no one knows you are interested, the chances are that you will not be considered. Getting ahead on the job takes more than merely doing a good job. You may have to re-state your accomplishments to your boss, and explain how the organization has benefited from your ideas and suggestions and will only benefit further by giving you greater responsibilities and duties.

When it comes down to the final interview, take note of the suggestions we make in this chapter and Chapter 5. Let your self-confidence and past achievements shine and if all goes well you will get that promotion!

The role of loyalty

Unfortunately, getting a promotion can often be a competition. You will have to fight for what you want – but fight fair. Loyalty plays an important role in getting a promotion. Contrary to what we see on television and in the movies, back-stabbing tactics will not get you very far in the real world. Being a loyal employee, co-worker or supervisor will only make advancement in the workplace easier. But remember the difference between loyalty and overkill. You do not have to be everyone's best friend. It is more important to be well respected than well liked.

Wrapping up the interview

You will nearly always be asked if you have any questions, or further information to impart that you believe may assist you to get the job. Make sure your questions are real ones and show off your intelligence. If you believe that some vital information about yourself has not been covered either in your application form or in your other answers, then add the extra information. Make it a crisp presentation.

Don't ask questions about the details of personnel policy (although it would be in order, for instance, to ask whether there is a flexible working hours system or hotdesking, this is not the moment to ask for a detailed account of the method used to run the system). On the other hand, if the situation is appropriate, you might want to ask what happened to create the vacancy you are hoping to fill. Did the last person get promoted, resign, take a career move or get sacked? The answer could be revealing, as could knowing whether there are any major new areas of work forthcoming or knowing about the organization's promotion policy and commitment to professional personal development. Remember that although the interviewers are asking the questions, they should be telling you enough to decide whether you want to work for them if they offer you the job. They will be saved expense as well as inconvenience if you find out at the interview that you could not bear to work for them, rather than only realizing this after six months' induction training courses.

The chairperson will formally bring the interview to a close and should tell you when the results of the interviews will be sent to candidates. If there is to be another set of interviews, then this information will also be given to you. The chairperson may shake your hand, so be prepared.

If the organization does decide to have a second interview the interview panel may well be different from the first panel, and you may find yourself being shown around the organization, meeting people and having 'mini interviews'.

In some sectors it is the done thing to send the chairperson a note of thanks as a professional courtesy. If that is the case in your field of work, use the notepad in your emergency kit to note his or her name at some suitable point in the interview.

Make your exit as neatly as possible. Don't appear over-anxious to leave and do try to remember where the door is – we have known interviewees in their haste try to escape through a cupboard door!

The do and don't checklist

Do:

- know something about the organization you are going to be interviewed for
- dress appropriately – you should know what is preferred by the organization
- arrange your timetable to arrive on or before time
- try to be calm

- think carefully about your answers – take time to answer, but not too long!
- give specific and full answers to demonstrate your skills
- know your strengths and weaknesses
- be prepared to answer questions about your hobbies
- be knowledgeable about current affairs
- have up-to-date knowledge about professional affairs
- watch your body language
- say if you do not understand a question – ask for amplification
- if from the interview questions you think the job is not for you, be brave and say so
- be prepared to ask questions about the job if you think that not enough has been divulged in the interview – after all you are the one who is going in to the new organization
- tell the interview panel if you think some vital information about you and your experience has not been covered.

Don't:

- be late
- be ill prepared
- be sarcastic
- be critical of your current boss or organization
- fidget during the interview
- generalize when giving your answers.

Summary

In this chapter we have looked at many aspects of job interviews. You should have some clear ideas about these issues:

- how interviews are likely to be run (though there are always exceptions!)
- what interviewers will be looking for
- what other assignments and tests might form part of an interview
- the kind of answers that will help an interview to go smoothly
- the importance of body language and unspoken behaviour
- what you can (and should) say at the end of an interview – and when to keep quiet.

7

After the interview

In this chapter we are going to look at the aftermath of the recruitment or promotion interview, and all the things to consider:

- How did you perform?
- How do you use feedback effectively?
- How do you evaluate the job offer?
- Do you really want the job or promotion?

In Chapter 6 we said that interviews are, for many people, the most stressful part of their career development, but for many others the post-interview period presents another bout of stress.

Obtaining feedback about your performance

Either before an interview starts or at the conclusion, the chairperson or interviewer may offer you feedback after the interviews are over. If this is not forthcoming, then ask if providing such feedback would be possible. You should try to get as much feedback as possible about your performance. Ask about the key points that determined how decisions were made, where you may have gone wrong, how you can improve next time, what impressions you gave and how you can manage these more effectively in the future. Keep a log of what you have learned, then take action to remedy any faults. Remember that practice makes perfect!

In your log construct a list of qualities by which you would wish to be seen, such as being determined, having a can-do attitude, being a good team worker, being self-motivated, and so on, then ask colleagues or your mentor how they see you. If there is considerable discrepancy between their idea of you and the list you have compiled, then ask how you can alter your behaviour for the better.

Evaluating the job offer

If you are fortunate enough to be offered the job that you have recently been interviewed for, you are faced with a difficult decision and must evaluate the offer carefully. Fortunately, most organizations will not expect you to accept or reject it immediately. There are many issues to consider when assessing a job offer.

Will the organization be a good place to work? Will the job be interesting? Are there opportunities for advancement? Is the salary fair? Does the employer offer good benefits? If you have not already figured out exactly what you want, the following ideas may help you develop a set of criteria for judging job offers.

The organization

You will have a reasonable amount of knowledge about the organization already to help you decide whether it is a good place for you to work. Factors to consider include the organization's business or activity, financial condition, age, size, and location and training opportunities.

Press releases, company newsletters or magazines, and recruitment brochures can also be useful. Ask the organization for any other items that might interest a prospective employee. If possible, speak to current or former employees of the organization.

Companies and many public sector organizations produce annual reports and other documents that give this information. If you cannot get an annual report, check the library for reference directories that may provide basic facts about the company, such as earnings, products and services, and number of employees. Stories about the organization on websites, and in magazines and newspapers can tell a great deal about its successes, failures, and plans for the future. However, it probably will not be useful to look back more than two or three years for information.

Does the organization's business or activity match your own interests and beliefs?

It is easier to apply yourself to the work if you are enthusiastic about what the organization does. This may have been a contributory factor in why you applied in the first place.

How will the size of the organization affect you?

Large organizations generally offer a greater variety of training programmes and career paths, more managerial levels for advancement and better employee benefits than small ones. Large employers may also have more advanced technologies, but jobs there may tend to be highly specialized.

Jobs in small organizations may offer broader authority and responsibility, a closer working relationship with top management, and a chance to see clearly your contribution to the success of the organization.

Should you work for a relatively new organization or one that is well established?

New businesses have a high failure rate, but for many people the excitement of helping create a company and the potential for sharing in its success more than offset the risk of job loss. However, it may be just as exciting and rewarding to work for a young firm that already has a foothold on success.

Does it make a difference if the organization is private or public?

An individual or a family may control a privately owned company and key jobs may be reserved for relatives and friends. A board of directors responsible to the stockholders controls a publicly owned company and key jobs are usually open to anyone. Work in the public sector is often governed by rules that ensure that recruitment is seen to be fair and open. This extends in particular to ensuring that there is no discrimination on any grounds such as disability, race, age, gender or sexuality.

Is the organization in a sector with favourable long-term prospects?

The most successful organizations tend to be in industries or sectors of the public service that are growing rapidly.

Nature of the job

You need to understand completely what a job offer really contains. Ask to see the job specification details and if necessary discuss them with a member of the staff. Even if everything else about the job is attractive, you will be unhappy if you dislike the day-to-day work. Determining in advance whether you will like the work may be difficult. However, the more you find out about the job before accepting or rejecting the offer, the more likely you are to make the right choice.

It may be that actually working in the sector and, if possible, for the organization that attracts you, would provide considerable insight. You can gain work experience through part-time, temporary, or summer jobs, or through internship or work–study programs while in school, college or university, all of which can lead to permanent job offers. And all of these are ways in which you can find out about long-term prospects, or discover that this sort of work is not really for you and be pleased that you maybe had a lucky escape.

Where is the job located?

If the job is in another area of the country, or indeed in another country, you need to consider the cost of living, the availability of housing and transportation, and the quality of educational and recreational facilities in that section of the country. Even if the job location is in your area, you should consider the time and expense of commuting. It is vital to look into this in detail. Will you want to be away from your friends and relatives?

Does the work match your interests and make good use of your skills?

The duties and responsibilities of the job should be explained in enough detail to answer this question.

How important is the job within this company?

An explanation of where you fit in the organization and how you are supposed to contribute to its overall objectives should give you an idea of the job's importance.

Are you comfortable with the hours?

Most jobs involve regular hours – for example, 37 hours a week, during the day, Monday through Friday. Other jobs in the information world may require night, weekend or holiday work, although this should be clearly stated from the outset. In addition, some jobs routinely require overtime to meet deadlines or sales or production goals, or to serve customers better. Consider the effect the work hours will have on your personal life.

How long do most people who enter this job stay with the company?

Use your network to find out if there is a high turnover that can mean dissatisfaction with the nature of the work or something else less than satisfactory about the job. Of course, it might mean that the organization's training is so good that people get promoted quickly, or find other work in the sector using the skills they have acquired.

Opportunities offered by the employer

Remember that a good job offers you opportunities to learn new skills, increase your earnings and rise to positions of greater authority, responsibility and prestige. A lack of opportunities can dampen interest in the work and result in frustration and boredom. The organization should have a training plan for you. What valuable new skills does the organization plan to teach you?

The employer should give you some idea of promotion possibilities within the organization. What is the next step on the career ladder? If you have to wait for a job to become vacant before you can be promoted, how long does this usually take? For example in UK government departments this is likely to take at least three years for the first move and ten years or longer for jobs at senior level depending on your skills and the opportunities. But recognize that it may not be possible to predict the future creation of new areas of work, or future constraints on expansion, so you may be given a combination of best estimates and aspiration.

When opportunities for advancement do arise, will you compete with applicants from outside the organization? It may be the policy of the organization that all jobs must be announced publicly. Can you apply for jobs for which you qualify elsewhere within the organization, or is mobility within the organization limited?

Salaries and benefits

If you have applied for a job in a private company wait for the employer to introduce these subjects. Some companies will not talk about pay until they have decided to hire you. In order to know if their offer is reasonable, you need a rough estimate of what the job should pay. You may have to go to several sources for this information. Try to find people who were recently hired in similar jobs.

Ask your tutors and the staff in placement offices about starting pay for graduates with your qualifications. Help-wanted ads in newspapers sometimes give salary ranges for similar positions. Check with CILIP or the recruitment agencies who have salary surveys for a number of sectors.

If you are considering the salary and benefits for a job in another geographic area, make allowances for differences in the cost of living, which may be significantly higher in a large metropolitan area than in a smaller city, town, or rural area.

Overtime

Learn the organization's policy about overtime. Depending on the job, you may or may not be exempt from laws requiring the employer to compensate you for overtime. Find out how many hours you will be expected to work each week (remember the European Union's Working Hours Directive) and whether you receive overtime pay or compensatory time off for working more than the specified number of hours in a week.

Starting salary

Also take into account that the starting salary is just that – the start. You may be told that the salary is on a fixed scale. UK central government leaves it up to individual departments and agencies to fix their own pay scales –there is no longer a national pay scale – but local government still has a recognizable structure of grades and pay scales, which are supplemented by various local allowances.

Your salary should be reviewed regularly; many organizations do it every year, sometimes dependent on the annual appraisal results. How much can you expect to earn after one, two or three or more years? An employer cannot be specific about the amount of pay if it includes commissions and bonuses.

Benefits can also add a lot to your base pay, but they vary widely. Find out exactly what the benefit package includes and how much of the costs you must bear yourself, for example what the pension plan is and what tax you are liable to pay on, for example, a car provided by your employer.

Summary

In this chapter we have looked at many aspects of how to decide whether to accept a job if it is offered to you.

You should have some clear ideas about:

- how you performed at your interview
- how to evaluate a job offer
- how to decide if this is the right job or promotion for you.

The references for this chapter and the previous one give just a taste of the reading material available on this topic. Entire books can be and have been written about how to get a new job, interviews and going for promotion, although there is perhaps less advice on weighing up the offers!

One last thought: when you have been interviewed a few times yourself, you will no doubt also have your own favourite tip. Why not exchange your tip for your colleagues' favourite interview tips, and widen your experience further?

8

Looking sideways . . . and back

This chapter tells you about:

- other opportunities that can come from using your skills to do other kinds of work with your own employer or another organization
- short-term postings
- taking secondments outside your organization
- losing your job
- temporary work
- going fully independent: the pitfalls, perils and pleasures of becoming self-employed
- setting up in business.

In the previous chapters we looked at the possibilities for developing your career by moving to permanent posts in other library and information services, and by continuing to do your present job from home. Now we look at the opportunities that can come from using your skills to do other kinds of work with your own employer or in another organization. We also look at the possibility of going fully independent and becoming self-employed.

Why looking at other opportunities in your organization may benefit your career

You may be surprised to read that we are suggesting that you may wish to move to other sections or departments within your current organization. However, working in the information and library services affords you the opportunity to view the activities of the various sections within your organization, and you may be able to gain useful experience not available in your own area, for instance, in the finance or personnel department. There may be opportunities to work on a specific project for a given period of time, or even to change jobs completely by, for example, working in the computer department, or moving into another department where library and information skills would be of benefit.

The way to make such a move will differ from organization to organization. You may need to enlist the support of the central personnel team or get your manager's personal endorsement. Be prepared to explain to others why your skills are relevant outside a library.

Short-term postings

Short-term opportunities for other work can arise when colleagues are temporarily absent on a project or when a vacancy needs to be covered until a permanent replacement is available. There can be benefits for all in your offering to work for a short time on another job in this way. From a manager's point of view there is the advantage that you already have knowledge of the organization and how it functions, probably know the staff and can be useful almost at once in the new area of work. You can, at the same time, acquire new skills that are of long-term benefit both to the organization and to yourself. If you are covering a vacancy, you can see whether you want to apply for it permanently.

For example, if your training officer goes on maternity leave, you could be a suitable candidate to replace her if your work has involved selecting training courses for your colleagues, or you can offer experience in organizing training events for your employer or your professional body. Working in training can be a great advantage for you in your earlier career. As you progress, training knowledge becomes an important competence – whether as a manager with responsibilities for staff training, or as an individual wishing to progress your own professional development. Libraries are often involved with Investors in People, the implementation of S/NVQs and specialist training. Another suitable secondment might be to a training centre, such as an open learning centre that makes extensive use of books, CD-ROMs, videotapes and other multimedia and audiovisual resources.

Some people are hesitant about leaving 'their' job for a secondment. There is a long track record in government library and information services of people who have been, in the jargon, 'outbedded' from the library and 'embedded' elsewhere in the department with great success.

Librarians acquire skills that enable them to work successfully in many areas. These are just some of the jobs that librarians have done successfully in public sector organizations in recent years:

- senior financial manager
- knowledge management developer
- manager of a minister's office in a government department
- minister's diary secretary in a government department
- exports adviser
- IT director
- contract manager for tendered services
- call centre service development manager
- records manager
- supporter of research specialists
- writer of research reports
- internet editor, author and webmaster (a growing area of opportunities for librarians and information scientists)
- intranet manager (same comment as for internet editor)
- chief executive's secretary
- public helpline personnel.

This is not to mention those senior figures in the world of public service, the arts, universities and so forth who have trained and practised as librarians! The opportunities are endless – librarians have people skills, information management skills and IT skills that make a winning combination.

Taking secondments outside your organization

Sometimes the opportunity may exist for staff to take secondments outside the organization they work in. Your organization may have links with other businesses or institutions and by making your interest known you could, for instance, work for a period in a charitable organization. If you are in a public sector body you might work with an organization that supports your own. Sometimes it is possible to work in a developing country when on sabbatical leave – see below – or to work with one of the international organizations such as the World Health Organization, the International Labour Office or the United Nations Environment Programme. There are also opportunities for exchange of library and information staff through organizations such as Libex: Bureau for International Library Staff Exchange, which recently moved from the Thomas Parry Library, University of Wales Aberystwyth to CILIP.

A further alternative is to work for Voluntary Service Overseas. Librarians are one of the categories of professionals that are urgently needed for work in developing countries. Working for VSO is a possibility both for young professionals at an early stage of their careers (for whom it makes a distinguishing feature of their CV) and for those at or near the end of a career, providing an opportunity to pass on their wisdom in a worthwhile fashion. The contact address for the current requirements is given in the references to this chapter.

If you have ideas about work elsewhere in the world you could advertise for an exchange in one of the prominent library and information journals in the country of your choice, or contact an 'opposite number'

– the university library, public library or industry sector information centre in a country you are interested in.

Losing your job

In a guide that is primarily about developing your job, it is a rather sobering thought that people who thought they had a sound career suddenly find that their jobs have disappeared. We referred earlier to some of the possible reasons why you might lose your job, such as global and local economic downturn, mergers, downsizing and so on. None of the words makes it any easier to face redundancy, even if information professionals may be better placed than most to read the warnings in advance. A number of commentators offer the advice that you should remember it was your job that was made redundant, not you, and that particularly for older workers (which nowadays means those over 35) temporary work is probably the best way back into work. Dealing with redundancy is a subject on which a number of useful printed guides are available; two further ways of getting help are to seek guidance from the specialist library recruitment agencies listed in the notes to Chapter 4, or to take advice from someone to whom it has already happened.

Temporary work

Many librarians work for considerable periods of their careers as temporary staff. Indeed, some employers adopt a policy of offering permanent contracts mainly or exclusively to people who have performed satisfactorily on short-term appointments. And, as we said above, doing temporary work is a way of returning to full-time work after leaving or losing another job. Being a temporary employee gives you some flexibility, such as being able to leave a bad job quickly. Be flexible yourself in return.

Short-term postings allow you to gain skills in different areas of work, since many employers will provide at least a basic level of training for temporary staff. After all, temporary staff will be of little or no use if not trained, even if their departure is predictable, perhaps in a matter of months. Posts are often advertised on internet mailing groups and web-based employment services. As we mentioned in Chapter 6, jobs often appear there before they appear in print.

Use employment agencies

Most of the employment agencies offer temporary work and this sort of employment is a good way of finding out about work in different sectors before making a final decision on a career path. Talk to the agencies and see which one you feel most comfortable with. If you come across someone who asks you for money to find you a job, go to someone who doesn't charge candidates. The main agencies in information and library services work don't, and nor do plenty of others.

Treat the agency like an employer. If you look a wreck when you go to the agency, they are unlikely to send you to see their blue chip clients. Take our tips on dress and attitude and apply them at all times. Tell the agency if you are going to be unavailable for work, for example if you are taking a holiday. They may have work at short notice and will need to know if you are out of the country for three weeks – the agencies also have a living to make and need to know who is available to fill assignments on their behalf. You may need to decide quickly whether you want an assignment – because if not the agency may offer it to someone else while you decide whether to vanish for a month to the Andes. Employers employ temporary staff because they want their vacancies filled, not because they like paying agency fees!

Learn basic skills

Your employability as a temporary employee will be increased by possession of some basic skills, notably keyboarding and knowledge of common software – probably the Microsoft Office suite and in particular Word, Excel and PowerPoint. Look to see whether your skills make you suitable for posts not only in mainstream information work but also as a web or publications editor, knowledge officer, archivist or in another area that can make use of your abilities.

Update your CV

Make sure that these skills appear on the CV you lodge with the agencies or the one that they help you to develop. Remember to update your CV as you gain further experience; you will obviously need to do so rather more frequently than someone in a permanent position. Use positive terms and highlight your achievements. (If you are going to be with an employer only for a short while, that employer would prefer you to make an impact during that time.) The description will probably include a number of different jobs so you do not need to go to great detail about them: try to stick to a couple of pages unless you have exceptional experience to offer. Further details will come out in interview so go prepared to talk about the posts you describe.

Interviews for temporary posts

When you go to see an employer about a temporary position, you can probably ask more questions than we suggested were advisable in a permanent career interview. Get a feel for the place and whether you want to work there. And keep in the back of your mind the question of whether you would want to stay there if the post suddenly became permanent.

Going independent – the pitfalls, perils and pleasures

Deciding to go independent is a major career step and you should not underestimate the seriousness of such a move. Nevertheless there is a thriving market in independent information and library work that is slowly growing and developing into the new areas that we described in Chapter 2. The majority of independents describe themselves as 'consultants' but that can mean anything from being a freelance providing additional indexing from home, to being a fully fledged adviser on management and other practices in libraries and information units.

Many of the current independents chose to follow this path when faced with an unexpected (or sometimes planned) block in their expected career as an employee. Redundancy is a common and unfortunate reason for taking this path among younger people; older LIS professionals may find that after early retirement they can prolong their active careers through work as an independent.

You should also be aware that consultants are often called in to do jobs in cases when management does not want to get blood on its hands, so you may quite often be paid to say things that neither your temporary employer nor you find particularly pleasant. The article from *Program* cited in the references to this chapter (Griffiths and MacLachlan, 1987) describes a case study on the use of consultants in a government library. The references to that article include some helpful analyses of the role of consultants, among which Colin McIver's article (McIver, 1986), although now some years old, remains pithy and to the point, with a welcome streak of humour throughout.

Much of the advice about working from home applies to work as an independent, too – except of course that it is you who are now responsible for providing the wherewithal to operate the company. A concise guide such as this cannot set out in detail what you need to do. As local rules will vary you should check with your local authority and others about the implications of using part of your house as working premises. You should also think about getting advice from other professionals, such as accountants, particularly if you will be acting as principal partner or otherwise paying people who work with you, and also to advise you on the financial effects of designating part of your home as office space. We look at these questions in the next sections.

There is no room here for us to do more than outline how to make the decision to become self-employed, but you need firm answers to the following questions:

- What do you have to offer?
- Is there a market for your skills now and in the foreseeable future?
- For how long can you survive without an income? It is not unusual for six months to elapse after start up before you receive any money.

Self-employment often challenges people, and not everyone can succeed at it, for a whole variety of reasons. From experience we can give you some advice and guidance, and also some words of caution.

Setting up in business

It is important when you start your business that you get the best possible advice from government organizations, your bank and an accountant. In the UK there are locally held courses run by various official agencies such as Business Link, which can help you in the start-up phase of your business. UK online for Business provides advice on doing business electronically, and works within the same government department as Business Link. All the banks have excellent advice packages and can be useful in helping you to set up a successful information business. When trade is really moving ensure that your invoices get paid on time, but remember it costs you in time to chase unpaid invoices. Your cash flow projections will need to take account of the delays in getting payment from many sources: even if you have agreed standard terms and conditions, it often takes weeks to get money out of organizations for whom you have worked, and if you are involved in work with international bodies (such as European Commission projects) you are likely to be waiting to be paid for work that you may have carried out some months previously. You may also have to pay commission charges to convert payments from one currency to another, and if your business is large enough it could be worth holding a bank account in another currency such as the euro, either within the 'Eurozone' or with one of the UK banks offering this facility.

Keep a close watch on the state of your finances. Most banks now offer online or telephone access to accounts, allowing you to keep close checks on the flow of payments. Likewise, an excellent accountant is a must: she or he will be able to save you far more money than you pay in fees.

Partners and associates

Be careful about the choice of partners and associates with whom you may join to carry out a piece of work. If they are not up to it, then your reputation will suffer. Treat your associates in an ethical manner: you depend on them to represent you through their behaviour and their professional approach, but you also owe it to them to treat them fairly over issues such as remuneration and their share in any intellectual property that you create. Ensure equal division of workloads when working with a partner or partners, or you may finish up doing most of the work in your enthusiasm to get the job done well. You may decide that the best way of tackling this is to get a document setting out working guidelines drawn up by a legal professional so that everyone is clear about their position.

Professional ethics

Be careful about the type of organizations or companies you do business with, because it will not enhance your status to be involved with those that have a poor reputation. Even if you are desperate for a job, weigh up the pros and cons – would you be willing to work with an organization that you would not wish to show on your list of clients? These might, for example, be companies that are poor performers environmentally, or disregard the health and safety of their staff, or indulge in dubious financial dealings. You will need to think particularly carefully before entering new areas of work such as competitor intelligence where there is a fine line between ethical and unethical behaviour, and where you may come across unscrupulous actions on the part of other companies or organizations. CILIP's guidelines on ethical behaviour are being redrafted and we have provided further guidance about the revised code of ethics at the end of this chapter.

Equipment

Ensure that your equipment is robust, and that your telephones, answering and fax machines, and computer equipment are in good working order. If you are working to deadlines, the last thing you want is equipment that fails.

Keep a track on your consumables because the costs can soon add up, and ensure that your accountant knows how much you spend in these areas. However, much can be obtained free of charge at trade shows if you do not mind using other people's promotional materials as office notepads! If you start to distribute such goodies yourself, see whether your printer can produce materials that are equally suitable for your own purposes, such as notepads that show your full address rather than just a logo, so they can be used for short notes to clients or double as compliments slips.

Likewise ensure that when sourcing overheads, such as your telephone service, suppliers give you the best possible discounts. The range of offers from telephone service providers as they compete for customers is bewildering, and the arrival of broadband has added to the complication. Shop around, contacting not only BT and your local cable provider (if you have one) but also the other telecommunications companies ('telcos') that offer deals, and keep an eye out for better offers. Where there are discounts on frequently called numbers, you can usually make your internet service provider (ISP) a member of the calling circle – it doesn't have to be someone you can speak to! But be careful as most telcos exclude ISP numbers from your free calls allowance, or else you need to be on a special deal to include them.

Don't forget that you will need to insure your equipment, as most domestic policies will not cover it, and that professional liability insurance will provide indemnity against claims for damages arising from your advice. Few companies offer this class of insurance, but CILIP offers access to tailored policies as a benefit of membership.

Reusing work

Keep copies of all your reports, both in paper and computerized format, because it is possible that some work can be reused. You may be asked to keep copies of reports as part of a contract, as a form of back-up for the client. Under UK copyright law, you hold the copyright in work that you do unless you assign it to the client through the contract that you agree. While many clients have now become aware of this, and seek to transfer all intellectual property rights to themselves as a condition of contract, investigate whether you can retain the right to describe the work in general terms without identifying your client. Otherwise you could be at a disadvantage should you wish to base a professional article on your experience. You should also be clear whether your clients will allow you to name them when pitching for new business, or will only allow you to identify them as 'a large pharmaceutical company' or some similar phrase. Make sure all this is recorded and that both parties have a copy of what is agreed.

Being independent, but working away

If your independent work takes you away from base, then do ensure that someone has access to your office and can retrieve information, receive and send faxes, deal with telephone calls, read e-mail and answer machine messages – and will return them as necessary. It is all part of customer care and projects a professional image. With the rapid growth of mobile telephone technology, it is relatively simple and not unduly expensive to maintain contact with clients. By using internet cafés, you can contact your staff, partners and customers by e-mail through your regular ISP or via services such as Hotmail or Yahoo! Mail, although you would be wise to ensure that you close the browser or clear the cache of the machine you are using before the next customer takes over, in order to ensure the privacy of your mail.

Extending your network and your skills

You must constantly extend your network by going to meetings, seminars and conferences. This goes for all information and library workers, but in particular for those working independently because 'seeing, being seen and talking' to other professionals are crucial to gaining future work. It is estimated that over 80% of new work for small and medium enterprises comes from contacts and repeat orders.

Keep up to date with your professional development. Take every opportunity to extend your networks; the wide range of offers of work that are available in other European countries provides one obvious source of new contacts and development for professionals in the UK and other EU members, since there are few restrictions on travel, work, or the mutual recognition of qualifications.

Getting the work

Obviously in a book of this size we cannot give you chapter and verse on how to get a continuous flow of work but when you are meeting a company representative always be well prepared and ready to act and think 'on your feet'. These agents may also want to extend discussions when they realize what you are capable of giving them as an informational professional.

When agreeing to a job ensure that your client organization's representative clearly understands:

* what they are getting for the price
* your day rate
* your expenses, including any hotels, etc.
* the overheads involved – you may need to quote a percentage for administration costs.

When agreeing to a job, record these details in a contract. You could offer flexibility through a lower day rate if the job covers a long period of time.

The pleasures of independence

Working independently brings many pleasures. There are no bureaucratic interventions that take time and effort to deal with. There are no longer the regular but unnecessary meetings that many organizations demand their staff attend. You can choose to work when you want to, when to stop and start, to work early or late in the day, or even at night! You can choose to have a holiday tagged onto a job, something that may be very difficult when working as a full-time employee for an organization. Being self-disciplined is essential, particularly when you are solely responsible for getting a project finished on time.

Scott Adams, creator of the Dilbert cartoons, observes that independent consultants have often made a deliberate choice to follow this career path. They get to choose their colleagues, and do not have to carry out many of the personnel-related tasks that ensue from being an employee or a manager. Especially if they are working to supplement other income, they can reject unattractive assignments, or walk away from projects that are not earning their keep or are causing more stress than they are worth financially. (However, it would be as well to ensure you never want to go back to that company or sector if you do this other than by mutual agreement: word gets round.)

Other benefits of working independently include the freedom (and the time) to think, to plan ahead, not to have to 'toe the party line', and to be able to move into other interesting-looking areas of work. These benefits may never be possible for an employee, but are part of the way that the independent practitioner learns to extend his or her services and expertise.

Working independently can be highly recommended for those with determination and grit who wish to move from a successful information career in the public, academic, industrial or other sectors of information and library work.

Codes of ethics

At the time of writing (June 2003), CILIP's code of ethics is being revised, with the aim of completion by late 2003. A consultation draft of the revised code is available (www.cilip.org.uk/about/ethicscode.html), which draws on both The Library Association's 1999 code of practice and the work done by The Institute of Information Scientists, where the number of independent consultants in membership led to a particular emphasis on discussion of professional ethics.

A number of other library and information professional bodies publish their code of practice or professional ethics on the world wide web. A page on the IFLA website (www.ifla.org/faife/ethics/codes.htm) provides links to them. Although it does not date some of the entries, it is current (and had the text of the 2003 French code within days of its ratification). While legal, fiscal and other systems will vary from country to country, it is a reasonable assumption that you will be able to find guidance on most professional problems from one or other of them. International subject-specialist organizations may also provide answers; these include the Society of Competitive Intelligence Professionals (SCIP) (see www.scip.org/ci/ethics_issues.asp for links to codes of practice and articles discussing the ethics of gathering competitor intelligence) and the Association of

Independent Information Professionals (AIIP) (whose Code of Ethical Business Practice is at www.aiip.org/AboutAIIP/aiipethics.html). Finally, other information organizations also have codes of practice that may help you to compile your own or to decide to subscribe to one of theirs; examples include the American Society for Information Science and Technology (ASIST) (code of practice at www.asis.org/AboutASIS/professional-guidelines.html) and the British Computer Society (code of conduct at www1.bcs.org.uk/link.asp?sectionID=229).

Summary

After reading this chapter, you should be able to identify:

- how you could gain experience outside standard working arrangements
- how you could work in a professional capacity on an exchange or as a volunteer
- how your professional skills could be used in other areas of work
- whether you have what it takes to be a successful independent professional
- how you can get support and advice if you decide to work independently.

9

Other considerations in career planning

This chapter looks at a range of questions about your longer-term career. We ask:

- Are you happy with what you are doing?
- What really interests or motivates you?
- How do you take your skills elsewhere?
- Have you thought about being a 'serial temp' worker?
- How do you follow trends in pay?
- What other benefits does a package offer?
- How can you return to work after a break?
- Where do you want to be in three, five or ten years time?
- Have you got a real work–life balance?

Now that we have shown you how to plan your career, assess the jobs on offer, apply successfully for a job or promotion and to look for other opportunities are you really happy and satisfied with your lot? Do you get frustrated because:

- things don't happen as you would wish?
- the pace of development is slow?

- there are no real training opportunities?
- there is no advancement in your career?
- there is no 'buzz' about the place?

If you say 'often' or 'sometimes' to any of these, then it may be that you have been in your present job for too long and are literally marking time. You could be too comfortable but getting nowhere and lacking the sense that you are fully achieving what you really want to do. (See our advice on the duration of a job in Chapter 2.) But we do accept that some people just want to slip slowly into old age!

To help you out of this dilemma we are going to look at a number of factors that should influence you to think about whether and how to move on.

What really interests or motivates you?

It is no bad thing to want to try other areas of work. Indeed it is stimulating and challenging to spread your wings and move into other sectors. The authors have worked in a wide range of information services, starting in public libraries, and can confirm these statements through personal experience. If you get bored with your daily work perhaps it is time to move on. This needs preparation. See the earlier chapters in this book, especially Chapter 2, to start you thinking.

Case study 4: A blend of new skills in electronic publishing

You enjoy using your skills and want to get more involved in projects that will extend these skills. There may be major initiatives such as establishing an intranet where you want to get more experience. No doubt you have upgraded your IT skills so you can put together web pages. You will have improved other existing information skills such as your writing skills, for instance by producing press releases, summarizing documents or writing answers to frequently asked questions.

If you haven't upgraded your skills in this way you might take relevant training at your local college or university if your organization is not geared up to providing the training in-house. Identify day or evening classes and make a proposal to the training officer. By doing this training you have established that you are in charge of your own development and career. You are also acquiring skills that you know are rare in your organization and this puts you at an advantage when the intranet is proposed.

In fact you can then propose the idea!

Case study 5: How new technology is changing the way in which cataloguers work

More recently, some new products and product developments are offering a change in the environment in which cataloguers and database compilers may work. The technology is available, or in development, to allow cataloguers to access bibliographic records, the internet and the primary bibliographic tools from a personal computer at a remote site. Alternatively, if in a specialist area such as health and safety at work, the journals that need to be indexed could be delivered directly on publication to the indexer who will index the articles remotely into the database, and then send the journals back to the information service. This could be taken a step further, by making arrangements to receive a regular flow of specific journals that were needed to be indexed for the particular database from places such as the British Library Document Supply Centre. Using the internet electronic journals content pages is also another way of being able to catalogue and index items remotely.

Trends in pay

If you are working in an organization divorced from any national or regional pay structures you need to keep an eye on the salaries and other benefits offered in the information sector.

The Chartered Institute of Library and Information Professionals continues to issue guides to salary levels in various types of library. This information is of growing value even in the public sector, where the old standardized pay scales are being replaced by more flexible arrangements. It is no longer true that you will be offered the same pay for the same job across the sector, and you often have the chance to negotiate when taking up a new job.

CILIP is developing a strategy for the gathering and dissemination of accurate and reliable pay data. The long-term goal is to ensure that members' contribution to their workplace is appreciated and well-remunerated by their employers.

Useful websites in the US and Canada

If you are looking for work in the United States or Canada, we advise you to explore the websites of the Special Libraries Association (SLA) and those of the national library associations (the American Library Association and the Canadian Library Association). The SLA site also covers jobs currently being advertised, virtual advisers, and career disruption, as well as an assistance programme and technical support. You can find similar help from other national library and information professional bodies, many of which have extensive free content.

The SLA site contains extensive information going back over several years about salary levels and trends in the US and Canada. In the most recent survey reported, the SLA mailed questionnaires to a random sample of its membership in the US and to all regular and associate Canadian members in early April 2002. Of the 6038 surveys mailed out, 2778 returned were analysed and entered so as to ensure respondent confidentiality. You can find summary details at www.sla/org/content/memberservice/research-forum/salarysurveys/index.cfm. You can order copies of the full surveys from the SLA, and more detail is available online to members of the SLA.

They also offer a 'Career Services Online' in another part of their website on www.jobcontrolcenter.com, which they describe as 'the talent network for the information profession', offering job opportunities and career development resources that will (the site claims) give users the edge!

The SLA advises that 'as an information professional, a whole world of new possibilities is within your reach'. The SLA Career Services Online offers to be an essential tool for success in the years ahead. Not only can you search for leading-edge job opportunities, but you have access to invaluable career development resources that will give you an edge in the highly competitive New Economy.

The range of job titles from the SLA site at the time of writing makes an interesting collection. Apart from posts being available for Librarians, there are vacancies for Cyber-Librarians, Information Research Analysts, Media Archivists, Library Systems Engineers, Design Librarians and a Knowledge Manager/Content Coordinator.

Other features include the 'Career Connection', which matches job seekers and employers during the SLA's annual conference by allowing each to pre-register job requirements and vacancies. The website then acts as a broker and sets up meetings between the job-provider and the job-seeker at the conference.

Watching the media for jobs advertised

As our own surveys demonstrated, you also need to look constantly at job advertisements, not only for information on salaries, but also for information about the skills required for different job specifications in the information sector. As we saw above, the range and variety of job titles is long and various. Perhaps some of these terms could be useful when describing your own work – after all you can call yourself whatever you think is the most appropriate title! However, if you choose a less than common job title for yourself, be ready to explain to a sceptical interviewer what the term means; you should include a word or two of explanation on application forms about any of the more way-out job titles. But terms such as 'information architect', which were considered fanciful a short time ago, are now accepted mainstream job titles in the new economy.

Have you thought about being a serial temp worker?

Many people want complete independence and flexibility in their jobs and temporary work may suit them, particularly at various stages of their career. Some people enjoy the challenges of regularly working in different organizations.

It could be argued that someone in the same job for ten years has only a couple of years' real experience and has spent the rest of the period just marking time. Meanwhile, someone who has being in three or even more 'temporary' or short-term contract jobs may have a wealth of experience gained through working in different cultures and in various backgrounds. For some people being a 'serial' temporary worker may be the ideal. This means that this kind of worker will be able to work as and when time and perhaps financial requirements allow. Keeping up with professional development is still essential.

The corporate sector trends of downsizing and re-engineering have profoundly affected corporate libraries. Along with the act of downsizing came the trend to outsource many positions and services that were traditionally performed by permanent employees. Company managements have reduced their permanent head counts and overhead costs through outsourcing, claiming that it is more cost-effective, efficient and allows greater flexibility. In fact this is nothing new and librarians and information managers have used outsourcing for years and have found it effective when done correctly. In some organizations, the only way to hire additional personnel is by using temporary workers. It also gives information managers the opportunity to see how an individual performs in case a more permanent job arises.

To make full advantage of this style of working, and to convince potential employers that you are a suitable candidate to carry out the work they offer, you need to display flexibility and the ability to transfer lessons learned (rather than other people's data and information) to the new workplace. It is essential for you to keep up with your professional development when you are not likely to be with any employer long enough to take full advantage of this aspect of permanent work.

What other benefits does a package offer?

Remember pay is not the only thing to consider, and that any package you are considering may include health care, fees for training, generous holidays, insurance and pensions, and so on. Do look at the complete package. For instance, in some jobs, particularly in the electronic publishing industry, no pensions are paid by the employers so what may seem a generous salary could be compensating for lack of pension. We advise that you will need to make sure that you have a personal pension plan if you intend to move around. Even if you intend to work in the public service throughout your career, there are different rules on contributions to the schemes in different parts of the sector that make it difficult to compare salaries and conditions. And remember to look at such far off things as the age at which a pension starts to be paid, or for that matter the age at which you are expected to retire! With the proposed changes to retirement pensions in the UK you could find yourself in a position where you need to cover five or even ten years between retirement and receiving your full pension. Remember too that retirement ages vary even further if you work in other countries – so you need to check carefully.

Other benefits may be offered such as travel allowances, car mileage allowances, a staff restaurant at low cost or luncheon vouchers. So when you are considering a package look to see how much all these other benefits add up and how (and whether) they will benefit you.

What lies over the fence?

If your interest is aroused but you have doubts about the upheaval that a job change may entail, such as moving house, do not be put off completely. You should satisfy your curiosity by at least measuring yourself against the market – read the advertisements, polish up your CV and apply for a range of jobs in which you are interested (and which, preferably, you would take if offered). The response to your applications will tell you how you match up to requirements elsewhere and will put you in a position to decide:

- whether you could take another job;
- whether you need more training or development; or
- whether your present job is not so bad after all.

All this information at little or no cost!

Returning to work after a break

We want to give some words of encouragement to those who are considering returning to work after a break, and are wondering how they are going to cope with the job (and a job market) that seems to have changed beyond all recognition since their departure.

There is a range of reasons for being away from work. Most can be planned for at work – maternity leave, sabbaticals and in-service further education, for example, can be written onto the planning calendar – but sometimes absence is unplanned, such as long-term sick leave. We think the advice in this section is useful also for people being seconded to other organizations (see Chapter 8), and for people who are posted overseas as part of their career. In the rapidly changing world of work, being away from the office for one year may bring problems, but a three-year absence in an office with a different culture and climate can make a return to the home base seem daunting.

Keeping in touch while absent

First we suggest that before any career break starts arrangements are made for you to receive staff circulars or newsletters. If you are connected to e-mail from your home it may be possible to arrange for you to be able to receive all this information through your computer, and to keep a record without gathering a heap of papers. This will keep you in touch with the ebb and flow of changes in your organization. You might consider doing some work from home, perhaps helping in emergencies, particularly if you can meet any security or other checks that may be required.

You should try and keep in touch with the team leader and other members of staff about the developments that are taking place in the service. Ask to see major documents such as the specifications of a new system being brought into the information services during your career break.

Keep in touch and keep your professional skills up to date, even to the extent of going on a training course. Ask if it is possible to spend a short period at the office every few months, if your circumstances allow this. Ring the personnel office, and ask them to update you on major events in the organization. If you are unpaid during your absence, remember the low cost of maintaining personal memberships of the professional bodies, and the news and information they bring.

When you go back

Bear in mind that organizations (and their information services) alter track. Do a mini-audit of your employer before you go back to work. Once you have decided on your return to work date, try and visit the information service for a couple of 're-acquaintance days'. These will give you an appreciation of what is where, who is who (there are bound to be newcomers in the staff while other familiar faces will have left), and any changes to the nature of work. (The classic example is the arrival of the internet – what would you have needed to do to catch up if you had started a five-year break as the internet explosion was just starting?)

When you go back, don't panic . . . remember that you have a lot of experience already, and you will be surprised how quickly you get back into the swing of things. Remember everyone has the same feelings after being away for a long time, whatever the reason. But there probably has to be some adaptation on both sides.

Ask yourself whether your habits have changed since you left. (Are you a late bird instead of an early one now, or will you need to leave early to deal with family issues? If you have been ill, has it affected your ability to do any of your tasks?) You may need to take care that everyone in the office understands this, and that any changes are not seen as undue favours or as evidence of diminished performance. People may be looking actively for changes in your habits and knowledge, so you may find that you are in effect having to prove yourself to the team all over again from the beginning. Remember, while you were away, someone else had to learn about your job and do it to something like your own standard. You now have to take it over again, and that will involve talking to the 'caretaker' to find out what changes took place in your absence. You will need tact and other interpersonal skills.

If you have been on long-term training, do not foist your new knowledge onto everyone! Getting on with the job and looking for an 'early win' by using your skills are far more effective ways of settling back than by going on at length about new theories and ideas. Harking back to your absence is not a good idea generally. Pass round the family photographs, tell people what it was like in a distant country, but don't make it the main point of your day. And try not to talk about your operation or list your health complaints twice a day!

If it helps, ask whether it is possible for you to work part-time, job-share or even work on a temporary basis.

Flexibility

A common quality mentioned in job advertisements is flexibility. Now this may be no more than a euphemism for shift working, but it may also signal that the employer is willing to look at alternative ways of working. This may enable them to avoid losing valuable trained staff who, for example, have new family responsibilities, or (as we saw in the last section) return to work full-time after illness, when full-time working may present too great a burden at first.

Employers recognize that they have as much to gain as the employee by taking a flexible approach to these problems. Flexible working hours, part-time working, home working, provision of workplace crèches or job sharing are some of the ways in which the demand for flexibility is being tackled.

Your manager (or you as a manager) will need to obtain agreement at senior levels in your organization to these changes, but this is becoming far easier than was the case even a few years ago. Fairness is essential. Not least, for those areas where both flexibility and fairness are built into the law (such as on issues of disability), the system must be seen to be beyond reproach. Finally, the system must also allow employees to demonstrate that they are being equally fair and flexible – for example, by ensuring that they can be reached at all times when they are meant to be on duty.

Where do you want to be in three, five or even ten years' time?

Depending on your age, you will give different answers to this question. Likewise, the answer will depend on your lifestyle and your quality of life requirements. We are reminded of the 35-year-old who just wanted to finish work as soon as possible to do his own thing. At each appraisal he reiterated his desire, which he managed to achieve some 15 years later!

For those who are more career minded we suggest that you should not hesitate to move jobs every three years or so, including internal moves. You may wish to stay longer, of course, if the job changes significantly or there are other compelling reasons.

So, where do you want to be in three, five or even ten years' time? Your ideas should now be taking shape, particularly if you are keeping a close watch on the leading-edge developments that surround the information industry. Who would have thought that four years ago information people would be running their organization's intranet, or managing the corporate knowledge base? Being one step ahead of the game gives the information professional a certain advantage.

Have you got the work–life balance right?

Work–life balance may be about adjusting working patterns. Regardless of age, race or gender, everyone should search for a rhythm to help them combine work with their other responsibilities or aspirations.

Increasingly, employers are developing a wide range of work–life balance options, covering flexible working arrangements and benefit packages. Here are just a few:

- *Flexi-time* lets people choose when they work, usually outside the agreed core times. This means staff can vary their start, finish and break times each day.
- *Staggered hours* mean employees can all have different start, finish and break times. This allows employers to cover longer opening hours. It also offers employees more flexibility, as long as they're consulted first.
- *Time off in lieu* is when employees take time off, in agreement with managers, to make up for extra hours worked. It's often used to compensate employees who attend meetings in the evenings.
- *Compressed working hours* let people work their total number of hours over fewer days. For example, you can work full-time hours over four days a week instead of five, or work nine days a fortnight instead of ten.
- *Shift-working* allows employers to maximize the use of their plant or facilities by letting staff work one after another through a 24-hour period. Some businesses are realizing that longer opening hours and more

flexible shifts mean everyone has more choice. Public libraries have used a variant of shift-working for many years to maintain their evening and weekend opening hours. Now several libraries are experimenting with 24-hour opening (at least to the extent that a working area with computers and perhaps a restricted reference stock is available at all times). Shift-working offers a means of ensuring that users have professional support for as long as possible throughout the library's opening period. It can be combined with other arrangements such as teleworking (see below), where staff on call (via a mobile phone) are able to log into the library systems from their remote location in order to deal with users' problems or to fix technical faults.

- *Shift swapping* lets staff negotiate their working times and shifts among themselves, while keeping the needs of the business or service in mind.
- *Self-rostering* involves working out the number of staff and type of skills needed each day, then letting employees put forward the times they would like to work. Shift patterns are then compiled, matching staff preferences to the required staffing levels as closely as possible. Self-rostering is used in some hospitals and care services.
- *Annualized hours* mean that total working hours are calculated over a year rather than a week. This means people can work according to the peaks and troughs of activity over the year.
- *Job-sharing* involves two part-time employees sharing the duties of a post normally carried out by one person. Job-sharers divide pay, holiday and other benefits. One possible complication is that if another position becomes vacant then either the sharers must apply for and be awarded the post together (and that means that they both need to be promoted together), or else find a new partner for their existing job if only one of them is promoted.
- *Term-time working* makes it possible for permanent employees to take unpaid leave during school holidays.
- *Working from home* has been made easier with the advent of new information and communications technologies. It is possible for all kinds

of work, such as translation, indexing and abstracting and report writing.

- *Teleworking* involves working at home and using a telephone and computer to keep in touch with the home institution. As we mentioned above, it can be combined with other flexible working options, and allows on-call members of staff to log in as and when required at night or weekends in order to deal with problems. We have heard of people on call who have dealt with technical faults at their library from a cyber-café in their holiday resort!

- *Breaks from work* are often a result of maternity or parental and paternity leave, but some employers also offer unpaid career breaks and sabbaticals.

- *Flexible and cafeteria benefits* include childcare information or vouchers, funding and time off for learning, pension or insurance contributions, laundry services, use of staff facilities, and in-house medical and dental care. 'Cafeteria benefits' means that employees can pick and choose those benefits that best suit their needs.

Summary

In this chapter we have looked at:

- how to be sure you are doing what you really want to do
- ways of getting nearer to your goal and ways to decide what to do next
- how to get back into work if you decide to take a break
- setting yourself goals three, five and even ten years ahead
- dealing with your work–life balance, including many ways of working flexibly.

Now it's your decision

We hope that these chapters have been useful to you, whatever stage you are at in your career. We are sure that armed with all this information you will make the right decisions about your future career. May we wish you luck and as much enjoyment as we have from our careers, which are still as interesting and stimulating as ever.

10

Career case studies

We conclude with some invited case studies that show just a few of the many paths that information professionals take in the course of their careers. They show a variety of ways that people move – Pat Gallaher moved to another continent; Irja Laamanen moved from subject specialism to information specialism; our American colleague shows how it is possible to move between different sectors; and Jan Parry describes her varied work in government libraries.

We asked our colleagues a number of questions:

1 When you started in information work did you have a definite 'career plan'?
2 If so, does it match where you are now?
3 What or who influenced your different career moves?
4 Looking back, would you have done anything differently?
5 Are there any reasons why you stayed in your particular sector of the information industry?
6 What are the skills you think that have helped you in your career? How often did you need to enhance them?

Here are their responses.

Pat Gallaher (née Gowers), Australia

I have never had a career plan. I have taken opportunities as they arose and enjoyed many diverse positions as a consequence; this includes self-motivated career changes and taking opportunities for advancement. Many people have been mentors or provided inspiration, including:

- my mother, who worked in a public and hospital library, and encouraged me
- in special libraries, where my career started, staff of the Sheffield Interchange Organisation, especially Angela Allott and Les Tootell, also David White, Joyce Spurr and Sheila Pantry
- in Australia, Margaret Findlay, Leslie Symes, Ali Sharr, Lennie McCall, Margaret Medcalf, Betty McGeever and many others.

I have enjoyed my life in libraries enormously; the diversity has been a constant challenge. Circumstances have affected the last stage of my professional career. Living in relatively isolated small communities in Western Australia (WA), the opportunities were in public libraries not specials. I really enjoyed special library work, but have found great satisfaction in working in public libraries too. Making a difference by providing people with relevant material to enrich their lives is a great privilege. I think it is helpful to have:

- an interest in people and a desire to provide good service
- an inquisitive nature – good 'detective skills' can be essential to acquire the information required
- tenacity and determination, and a willingness to lobby and fight for continual improvement
- good promotional skills
- an interest in new developments and techniques
- the commitment to attend conferences and to read professional literature.

I certainly believe that libraries change lives. Libraries have changed and enriched my life during my career, which spanned more than 40 years and two continents, before I retired in 2000. After working for about seven years as a laboratory technician at Sheffield University, UK, I changed direction and ventured into special librarianship in the engineering and steel industries, while studying at night school. I qualified in 1965, the same year as I emigrated to Sydney, Australia, where I worked in the Defence Standards Laboratory for about three years before my first job in a public library (Mosman in Sydney).

After a period of travel, in Australia and overseas, including UK where I worked again in Sheffield at Granville Technical College, I returned to Australia in 1973. I spent most of the rest of my career in public libraries, eight years in the Pilbara region, famous for its iron ore, but also for spectacular scenery and a hot dry climate. In 1981 I was fortunate to be appointed as City/Regional Librarian in Geraldton, about 450 km north of Perth. Geraldton area now has a population of about 32,000 and became a city in 1988, an exciting year, when the Queen visited us (I arranged for a leather-bound book as a gift for her) and there were many celebrations. My time in Geraldton was a time of great change and there were always new opportunities and challenges to pursue to provide the best service possible for our rural community, which had only one public library available.

The State Library Service of WA was based on the County Library system in England and has been very successful for a large area so sparsely populated. Francis (Ali) Sharr's vision has provided residents of WA with a library service to be proud of. His contribution since he emigrated from Manchester in 1954, to his death in 2002, was enormous and he was highly respected throughout Australia by the library profession.

As Regional Librarian for the Geraldton (Mid West) region, I had an advisory responsibility for 27 small libraries under the control of local governments, in a region of about one-fifth of WA's total land area. I was expected to visit each one annually and arrange a meeting once a year for library officers (mostly untrained) to meet each other and relevant staff of the State Library, which provides the resources and support services such as interlibrary loans. They discussed issues relating to their libraries and shared skills and ideas. This was a most enjoyable part of the work and over the 20 years I travelled more than 26,500 km, along roads that varied from gravel to narrow bitumen and along the highways, and became very familiar with the Mid West region and its problems of isolation and lack of services. One area, the Murchison, which had seven of the libraries, required travel by light aircraft, which was always exciting and sometimes scary, especially if there were thunderstorms in the area. I was full of admiration for the dedication and innovative ideas of many of the library clerks in these very small communities and learned as much from them as they did from me!

As Regional Librarian I was also required to visit Perth monthly to attend meetings and select stock to add to our collection. These were important networking opportunities with other professionals to discuss issues affecting us all. Of particular importance were the various groups such as the Regional and Country Librarian's Group, WA Local Government Librarians Group (WALGLA), as well as the WA sections and branches of the Australian Library and Information Association (ALIA). The support of the State Library of WA to libraries in rural and remote WA has been fundamental to our success; without its support we couldn't have achieved what we did. Also important to country libraries was the generous assistance given by larger metropolitan library systems, which provided us with promotional material and activities for holiday programmes. It was many years before we could employ someone to take responsibility for children's activities, so we greatly appreciated this support.

The increased use of technology affected and assisted us all. Despite inadequate resources and lack of technical expertise we were still able to take advantage of some new developments with encouragement and assistance from the State Library and some financial support from the City of Geraldton. The connection to the internet and the State Library's catalogue and website were essential in our efforts to provide an equitable information service to our community and this will be a continual challenge.

One of the strengths of the Geraldton Library is its local studies collection, which has grown and developed during my time as City Librarian, with the aid of an excellent Local Studies Librarian, and strong community support. Geraldton, a coastal city, is not widely known as a tourist destination, but has many unique attractions and significant heritage sites. Its documentary history is a great asset and the collection is heavily used. Several books have been published by or in association with the library, creating a wider awareness of Geraldton's role in WA history. The city's website, www.geraldton.wa.gov.au, which has links to the library site, may be of interest.

My love of the arts, nurtured as a teenager in Sheffield, has influenced my life in Australia too, and I have involved myself in various activities to enrich cultural life in rural Australia. I have served on many committees, local and state, to ensure that the needs of country people are recognized.

I consider I have had one of the most rewarding of careers, which has recently been capped by my appointment to the Library Board of WA, the policy-making body for the State Library of WA. I was elected to the Council of the City of Geraldton in 2000, so I hope to continue my support for library services in our community.

I have been awarded certificates of achievement, by ALIA WA Branch and WALGLA, and was immensely honoured to receive an Order of Australia Medal in the 2002 Australia Day Awards for my efforts for the arts and as a regional librarian.

Librarianship has been good to me and I feel privileged to have found such a rewarding profession and met some wonderful people along the way. I firmly believe libraries will continue to play a significant role in people's lives, despite the current emphasis on technology; dedicated librarians will always be needed.

Irja Laamanen, Finland

When I started my studies in genetics in the University of Helsinki, I planned to become a geneticist, and at about the same time I was asked to work part-time in our local library. I think this was because I had been, for very many years, one of the regular users of the library. So I could not resist that offer, and I worked there for three years. It was pleasant work and it was possible to earn some money, which I needed when I became pregnant during my first year of studies and my young family needed money to live. When I had proceeded in my studies the Librarian of the Institute of Genetics asked me to take care of the Library of Genetics during her maternity leave. So I got experience from working in a scientific library and also two weeks of training organized by the University of Helsinki to be able to take care of that library.

Mostly what has happened to me has not been deliberately planned. My studies have been planned. I had two possibilities: either to become a real scientist or, after working several years in libraries, to become more qualified in information studies. So after eight years of studies and with three children I had to decide either to continue my scientific career or to become a 'real' information person. I decided to take a course at the Technical University of Helsinki to become an information specialist. I did it and got a permanent job as a librarian in the Institute of Genetics. That was not enough for me. I wanted more. 'Hunger grows when you are eating.' I wanted to specialize as a real information person.

Many librarians and library heads and directors have had an effect on my library moves: the head of the local library; the head of the library of the faculty of agriculture and forestry; Professor Esko Hakli who was the director of the National Library of Finland; the former library director of the Finnish Institute of Occupational Health – Annaliisa Larmo, and so on. My very close friend, Marita Rosengren, who worked in the Library of Genetics before me, proceeded some steps ahead of me. She was a good example for me.

Looking back I do not think I would have done anything differently.

I am happy with my career and have achieved quite a lot, not only on my own but also through the help of the other people in the same sector. Networking is so important: you get strength, ideas and support. These are needed both when you are young and when you get older!

There are many skills needed in this kind of work – it depends on what you are doing. The accumulation of skills has been important. For example, one of the jobs I was involved in was as project leader. In the beginning I was afraid and I felt I needed more skills. I had been working in smaller libraries and the university library was huge; when Professor Esko Hakli asked me to become a project leader it was a very big challenge. I took it and grew a lot. Without it I think I would not be where I am now. It needed a lot of computer skills, communication skills, planning skills, project skills, and so on. So taking this one opportunity was a turning point for me and has helped in my subsequent work.

In my job I have to acquire skills and knowledge all the time. I think I will have to do it to the end of my life. That was one thing I realized even as a child. I am happy to have new challenges and opportunities. Without them I would be like a rolling stone.

Currently my job as Director of Information Services at the Finnish Institute of Occupational Health in Helsinki has brought me to the world of international occupational safety and health. Through this network I have been able to help other information specialists in different countries. My work in Eusidic is also important to me.

Curriculum Vitae

Qualifications

MSci University of Helsinki, with degrees in Genetics, Microbiology, Chemistry, Biochemistry, Statistics, 1978

University of Technology, Helsinki

Course of Information Science, information specialist degree, 1980–1981

University of Helsinki
Degree in Adult Education, 1997

Professional experience
Public library, library assistant, 1969–1971
Finnish Academy of Science, 1976, research assistant
Helsinki University, Department of Genetics, Librarian, 1974
Helsinki University, Medical Central Library, information specialist, 1975
Helsinki University, Department of Genetics, Librarian, 1980–1983
Helsinki University, Scientific Library, information specialist, 1984
Finnish Institute of Occupational Health, information specialist, 1985
Helsinki University, Library of the Faculty of Forestry and Agriculture, information specialist, 1986-1988
Helsinki University Library, VTLS project manager, 1989
Finnish Institute of Occupational Health, Helsinki, Director of Information Service Centre, 1990–

Experience
FIN-EST Twinning project, 2000–2002: my responsibilities were the developing of databases and library and information services at the Occupational Health Centre
Project leader, production of Safety CD-ROM discs, 1994–2000
Project leader, databank on information intensive work, 2001–2002, developing ongoing Partner in Worksafe project (EU, eContent), 2002–2004

Teaching positions
Lecturer in library and database user education for students of genetics and forestry and agriculture 1975–1988
Lecturer in database user education on occupational health, toxicology and chemical safety, 1990–

Language skills
Finnish, Swedish, English, understanding of German and some Italian and Spanish

Publications
40 articles, of which four were on genetics and the rest on chemical safety data and databases and informatics. Two posters presented in the ICOH conferences (Singapore 2000 and Brazil 2003).

Co-author:
Riihimäki, V., Isotalo, L., Jauhiainen, M., Kemiläinen, B., Laamanen, I., Luotamo, M., Riala, R. and Zitting, A. (2002) *Kemikaaliturvallisuuden Tiedonlähteet*, Helsinki, Työterveyslaitos. Also available at www.occuphealth. fi/ttl/osasto/tt/Kemikaalitieto/index.html. [Accessed 24 April 2003]
Tieto ja Tekniikka – Missä on Nainen? (2002) Various authors and editors include: Smeds, R., Kauppinen, K., Yrjänheikki, K. and Valtonen, A., Helsinki, Tekniikan Akateemisten Liitto TEK. ISBN 952-5005-67-4.
Den Tredje Nordiska Konferensen för Medicinska Bibliotekarier, Helsingfors 26.- 28.8.1991: föredrag och sammandrag av paneldiskussionen och gruppmötena (1992) Compilers: Laamanen, I., Luoma, A., Salmi, L., Helsinki, Bibliothecarii Medicinae Fenniae.

Member of
Finnish Research Library Association (http://pro.tsv.fi/stks/)
Chair of the Finnish Serials Group (Member of UK Serials Group)
EUSIDIC – council member and treasurer; representative of Finnish Society for Information Services (www.eusidic.org)
Finnish Society for Information Services; member of one workgroup (www.tietopalveluseura.fi)
Member of Zonta International: Club IV, Helsinki, Finland

Information specialist from the USA who prefers to remain anonymous

I did not have definite career plans when I started in information work 25 years ago but I knew I liked the computer aspect of the field and focused my graduate education in that area. I received a Masters of Library Science with a specialization in Information Science. My first professional position after getting my MLS was as a reference librarian in an academic library. The primary reason for choosing the academic community was simply because I liked the collegial and learning atmosphere of a university. At that point in my career I had little knowledge of special libraries and as a result did not explore career opportunities available in that sector.

In the sense that computers are everywhere and have changed not only the face of information services but also society, with the impacts of the internet, my original desire to work with computers does match my current situation. In terms of the collegial atmosphere, I have experienced that as well in the academic, government and corporate settings. It is an important component of my job satisfaction.

I would say that two individuals had major influences in my information career. The first was an undergraduate professor who taught Library Science. I took the course in my senior year basically on a lark and ended up really engaged in the whole concept of retrieving information and organizing knowledge. I feel this professor was responsible for my choice of information as a career. The second primary influence in my career was Sheila Pantry. Sheila opened up the international information community to me and provided me with numerous opportunities to work with information professionals on a global basis. In addition, I also feel that Sheila was directly responsible for enabling me to make the contacts needed to move into the corporate information world. She was the invited speaker at a Special Libraries Association local chapter meeting that brought in corporate attendees. At this meeting I was approached by one of the corporate information professionals who suggested I apply at her company. This ultimately resulted in employment at that company.

I wish I had moved into the corporate sector of special libraries sooner. I really enjoy working in the private sector where the bottom line is a strong influencer of how and what information services can be provided. It's a combination of business and information savvy.

I have worked in special libraries for 23 years and have found the work immensely satisfying. The intertwining of information skills with a specific subject expertise suits me.

Obviously, I think my computer skills have aided me in my career. Since computers change at a rapid pace, I continually look for opportunities to build skills in this area. But beyond that, I think that having good people skills are paramount in having a successful career. Since information provision is a service, we obviously need a very strong service orientation. We continually need to understand our customers and deliver information products that meet their needs. Good people skills are also essential for effectively managing others in their work so that they realize their full potential and are able to make their maximum contributions. I believe one has to continually enhance one's people skills, both through formal training courses as well as on a daily basis during interpersonal interactions.

I am very happy I chose information as a career and believe I would choose it again if I were starting all over. That being said, I see some significant challenges ahead for the profession. The widely held perception that 'everything is available on the Internet so why are information professionals needed?' is a significant threat to our existence. We need to continually demonstrate the value we bring to the institutions and clients we serve by providing high quality information in a user-friendly format and in a cost effective and timely manner.

Also, I think we will see an increase in the trend of special libraries in companies to outsource information services so they can focus on their 'core' business. The relatively recent phenomenon of high-tech knowledge work moving to lower cost locations such as India and the Philippines may have negative employment impacts on the information job markets in the US and possibly Western Europe as well. It's a rapidly changing world – we need to readily accept change and adapt accordingly.

Jan Parry BA(Hons) MCLIP, Performance and Change Manager, Private Office, Home Office, UK Government

When you started in information work did you have a definite career plan?
I started in information work as an administrative officer in a Government Information Services library at the Health & Safety Executive (HSE), Bootle. This was the most interesting work I had ever done while in the Civil Service and I decided I wanted to continue my working life with a career in the library profession. In order to do so I first needed a degree and so I took a three-year unpaid career break in 1988 in order to get one. (This was not an easy task financially as we had only my husband's low salary to live off and we had two growing daughters!) My career plan at this stage was to become professionally qualified to enable me to get promotion within the library that I worked in.

While at university I discovered that not only was I ambitious but that I had skills that were bursting to be free and I developed a healthy interest in computers. I realized that there were more opportunities in information work in London so my husband and I decided that we would be willing to move south in order to make a better life for the family. My career plan was now broadening.

After graduation in 1991 we moved to London to my first professional post as an assistant librarian in the Department of Health. I set myself personal goals and targets based roughly on promotion every five years. These were secret goals so I told nobody (not even my husband!); then if I failed to reach them, only I would know. My career plan was therefore to get promoted to Librarian grade within five years. This happened in three years but I was disappointed not to be offered the job I really wanted (note: this was a management decision and not my own!).

In order to make life more interesting and get new skills I moved sideways to a job working directly to government ministers. I used all my professional and managerial skills to help them organize and retrieve information but also learned budgeting skills and developed my staff management and IT systems skills.

I was in the right place at the right time, for once, when a new Labour Government came to power in 1997. While in opposition, they had made full use of new technologies to share electronic information and were surprised to learn that government had barely left the starting line. They needed an electronic briefing system and I was an information manager with experience in ministers' offices – an ideal candidate for the job of looking after the new system – so I was promoted to Senior Librarian. As the electronic briefing and information systems were gradually adopted by other government departments, in 2001, I took the opportunity of a sideways move to build a team of librarian content managers and IT specialists implementing the electronic briefing system in the Home Office.

In 2002 I passed an assessment centre for promotion to the next grade and was approached by the Home Secretary's office for the job of Performance and Change Manager. I now help ministers' offices modernize their ways of working by sharing best practice, improving information sharing and making full use of the electronic briefing system.

I have used all my professional skills and experience in all the jobs I have done. More importantly these skills are probably appreciated more in jobs outside the information profession because other people just don't know how to do the sort of things that come naturally to a librarian. We just don't appreciate ourselves enough!

Does it match where you are now?
I have more than achieved all the goals I set as I have actually been promoted four times in the last 11 years (and my last two promotions came well in advance of the targets I had set). I have actually reached what had been my highest expectations so I could sit back satisfied now, but that

would not really be me. The main thing is that any future promotions will be a bonus in comparison with my original target.

What or who influenced your career moves?

1　The Head of Information Services at the Health and Safety Executive (HSE), Sheila Pantry, who approved my three years' unpaid leave to take a degree and who recognized my talents.

2　The offer of a relocation package to move to London influenced my decision to stay in government library work. We would probably not have moved at all without this.

3　My decision to move from managing two libraries, a job that had been given to me, to different and more challenging work with ministers changed my career path and speeded up my promotion prospects.

4　My decision to move sideways to a different government department gave me more experience and new skills but also meant breaking out of my comfort zone.

5　My husband and daughters who have supported me through all the stresses and strains of each job application, interviews, new jobs and the long hours working for ministers.

Would I have done anything differently?

Not really. I wish I had not been so naive and 'green' about the 'politics' within the information profession. It took working in a job dealing with real politics for me to learn how the politics in any organisation works. You have to accept there is a system and work with it. Sadly, we have to accept that some job offers and promotions happen because of relationships or favouritism and not because you haven't got the skills and experience for the job or that you wouldn't do it well. In fact there are times when the people who didn't get the job would have done it better than the successful candidate so recruiters do get it wrong sometimes. Had I realised this earlier I would not have applied for every Librarian grade post that was advertised and I would not have beaten myself up for not getting them but on the positive side it did give me valuable interview experience and got me noticed.

Are there any reasons why you stayed in your particular sector of the information industry?
While at university I discovered an interest in computers and electronic information systems so I now combine this with communicating with people and making their working lives easier by organizing information and enabling them to retrieve it.

What are the skills you think that have helped you in your career? How often did you enhance them?
I think the skills that helped me in my career are:

- personality – excellent communication skills
- organizational skills
- initiative
- ability to understand what people need before they realise it themselves
- management skills
- feeling fear but doing it anyway – breaking out of my comfort zone
- project management skills
- assertiveness
- ability to see things from a customer's point of view.

I have probably gone on management training courses of various types at least every two years and at one point needed refresher assertiveness courses (and dealing with difficult people) annually, in order to help my own self-esteem.

I read journals covering change management, personnel management and information management.

I network a lot with old and new colleagues, and contacts I have made on training courses. This is an excellent way of learning from others and generally letting off steam!

Summary

It is difficult to provide a summary for this chapter in the way we have done for others. The lesson to be learned from the case studies is that there is no single right or wrong way to do your career planning, and no right or wrong path to take. The important things are that you are curious enough to consider and investigate opportunities, and that you take a more or less measured risk – depending on how comfortable you are or can afford to be with risk – based on what you find out. As an information professional you are in a unique position to do your homework on any opportunity that comes your way. Build your network of contacts and nurture it by sharing information with your peers and colleagues. Above all you can be pleased that you chose this career. It has been a long time coming and there are still many people to convince, but the breakthrough to the mainstream of business is taking place. Respected writers are telling the decision-makers, the movers and the shakers in all walks of life that they have undervalued their librarians for too long. What a pleasure to be part of the profession as its true value is realized at last!

Appendix 1

Typical questions on an application form

The form excerpts below show some typical questions that are found on an application form. Our comments point to common errors or loopholes in completing the application. Take care to ensure that your form is not ruled out or put to one side because you failed to do what was asked!

Application for Employment

Please complete this form in black ink or typescript and send it to the Personnel Manager at XYZ Co by the closing date shown in the advertisement. Please complete fully even if you send your CV as well.

Comment: Do what is asked. Black ink and typescript allow the employer to photocopy the application. If you are asked to write a letter in your own handwriting, do not type. If you are asked to send a CV, do not just send a short letter that is not backed up by detail of your career and skills.

You will then be asked a number of questions (not shown here) that will include:

- your name (including any other names you have been known by)
- your permanent address and its telephone number
- the address and telephone number where you can be reached (e.g. during a summer holiday)
- your date of birth
- your place of birth
- your nationality (and probably your immigration status if born outside the European Economic Area)
- whether you have any disability.

Education after age 14

School, college or university, dates, examinations taken and results

---

Comment: Note what is being asked for. Some forms ask for all schooling, some only for A-levels or degree level courses, depending on the level of the job. Examinations taken include the ones you failed! Remember that they appear on your certificates even if you obtained less than a C at GCSE or an E at A-level, so don't conceal them.

Employment information

Current or most recent employment

Name and address of employer; salary; dates of employment; type of work; reason for leaving

---

Comment: Be honest. Be positive. 'Better job' is probably acceptable in most circumstances as a reason for leaving and is better than 'Argued with manager'. If you did argue, the reference will show this – but most employers will delay asking for a reference until after you have been offered the post, so you do not have to air your differences in public at this stage.

Previous employment
Name and address of employer; salary; dates of employment; type of work; reason for leaving

Comment: The same comments as above apply. If you have held many short-term posts, you may run out of space. Complete a continuation sheet; refer in less detail to temporary posts some time ago; if you were an agency temporary, ask the agency if you can quote them as a reference instead; or call the personnel office at your prospective employer and ask for guidance.

If you leave in detail about a post a long time ago (more than, say, ten years) make sure it is relevant to the application. Make sure you enter details about the type of work, especially parts of it that seem to be relevant to what the new job involves.

Please say why you are applying for this post and what you think you can offer.

Comment: Write something; make it sensible. One of the most common reasons people give for any application is that the post is 'a challenge'. Concentrate on how the post matches your experience and skills, how it forms part of what you want to do in your career plan, and how you will bring skills, experience and enthusiasm.

You will usually get about a third to a half of a side of A4 paper for this section. Aim to fill the space without writing unusually small or large, and without writing anything unusually trite. Tell yourself that a machine could be reading your form before a human sees it, so your words should be positive and dynamic.

If you can't write anything sensible about the attractions of this job for you, and what you can offer, the chances are that it's the wrong job and you won't say enough to be selected for interview. Keep reading the vacancies listing.

Please give the names of two referees who can speak for your character, qualifications and experience. One of them should be your present or latest employer, if any.

Comment: Once again, read the statement, as it varies from form to form. If you have to give your employer's details and do not want them to know, look for a box against the referee's details that reads 'May we contact them now? Yes/No' and mark it accordingly.

Please give any dates when you are unavailable for interview.

Comment: Sometimes you can't help being unavailable, but you would be surprised how many people are called to interview on a day they forgot to tell the employer they were unavailable. We leave you to consider whether this goes down well with interviewers or not!

Please account for any time not otherwise shown on this form.

Comment: It is crucial that you do not conceal anything in reply to this question. If you went backpacking to India, it gives you something to discuss. If you were ill, or even detained in a prison establishment, then this needs to be indicated, within the rules that apply on admitting spent convictions or patient confidentiality. If the reason for your absence from the job market is significant it can be taken up later. In any case, there is no possibility of an offer being withdrawn later if you are straightforward about such matters.

Please make any other statement that you wish in support of your application.

Comment: Much as with statements to the police, you are not obliged to say anything but anything you do say may be used in evidence. So if you want to make a further statement about your knowledge, experience, or other matters, here is the place to do it. But if you are the kind of person who hates leaving blank spaces on forms, be sure that what you say warrants the effort both of saying it and of reading it.

Appendix 2
A possible CV for a library or information professional

Anne Applicant	• Don't write 'CV' at the top – it is unnecessary and some readers take exception to it.
Full name: Anne Eager Applicant	• Give your full name as it will be needed if checks need to be carried out.
Date of birth: 31 March 1972	
Address: 28 Ambridge Road, Borchester	• If you have a name that is used by both sexes, you might head the CV 'Mr Hilary Applicant' or 'Ms Leslie Applicant.' The same goes for less usual first names. If you want to be very formal you could say 'Sex: Female' or 'Sex: Male'
Contact address: 10 Bull Close, Ambridge	
Telephone: 029 3034 2341	
Fax: 029 3034 4312	• If you live at another address during the week, make sure the details are clear (and that you give a phone number where you will be!)
e-mail: annea@borset.gov.uk	• Check your e-mail regularly!

Education

BA (Hons) 2:1 in English Literature, University of Birmingham, 1994

A-level: English (A), History (B), German (A)

9 GCSEs

MLib University of Central England, 1996

- Give your academic history and professional studies. If you have an extensive career to present, you are unlikely to want to set out your GCSEs or O-levels in detail, or, perhaps, name your school. If you have an A-level in a language you claim to know, this would be useful to show in detail.

Experience

Borsetshire Library Service
Deputy librarian, Ambridge branch (1998 to date)
Graduate trainee, Borchester North branch (1997-1998)
Duties including lending and reference work, mobile library services and cataloguing.

Work experience
Library, Heavy Metalworks, Birmingham (1995)

Part-time employment
Checkout operator, Safeco super-market, Borchester (1994)

- List your experience in reverse chronological order. Employers' full addresses will be given if you fill out an application form, so save the reader's time here by giving brief details. Describe the duties in outline.
- Less detail is needed for early posts in an established career.
- Show other employment that reflects on your skills, eg working with the public as a supermarket employee.

Competences and skills

Service to the public. Professional skills including cataloguing. Organizing training events

- Pitch these towards any pointers in the advertisement that ask for particular knowledge or experience. Here is the chance to set out your stand!

173

Languages German (fluent written, spoken and read)	• Make sure you really do speak these languages! Give some indication of how fluent you are and in what situations. If you have a second language (such as an ethnic minority language) as a mother tongue, make this clear.
Publications Library services in the engineering industries of the Midlands (Thesis, UCE, 1994, unpublished) 'Engineering libraries in the Ruhr', *International Library Student*, vol 1, no 3, 1997, pp 12–17	• Many people have a thesis to cite these days even if they are not prolific authors!
Interests Orchid growing, visiting National Trust properties, running marathons	• Make these interesting! It will not add much of value to your application to list 'reading' as a hobby – unless of course you specialize in a relevant type of literature
Referees:	• Only quote them if they have already agreed to provide a reference!

Further reading, websites and organizations

Chapter 1 Scene setting: the challenges of today's employment market

Arnold, S. E. (1999) The Future Role of the Information Professional, *The Electronic Library*, **17** (6), (December), 373–5.

Blair, L. (2000) Beyond the Square: career planning for information professionals in the next millennium, *New Library World*, **101** (4).

Carrières de Bibliothécaires en Europe: dossier (2000) *Bulletin des Bibliothécaires Français*, **45** (1), 76–81. (Articles on library careers in Spain, the Netherlands and Belgium.)

Cheng, G. (2001) The Shifting Information Landscape: re-inventing the wheel or a whole new frontier for librarians, *New Library World*, **102** (1160/1), 26–33.

Current Initiatives in Librarianship and Information Science. Available at www.cilip.org.uk/info/gatewaytotheuk.html [maintained to date, accessed 10 April 2003].

Davenport, T. H. and Prusak, L. (1998) *Working Knowledge: how organizations manage what they know*, Boston, MA, Harvard Business School Press; paperback (2000), ISBN 1578513014.

Farmer, J. and Campbell, F. (1997) *Reaching Beyond the Plateau: identifying special librarians' transferable skills through learning pairs*, British Library

Research and Innovation Centre, BLR&I Report 46, ISBN 0712333118.

Funredes (2002) Available at www.funredes.org/LC/L5/ultimas.html [accessed 27 May 2003].

Griffiths, P. (2001) All that Glitters: the role of the information professional in handling rogue information in the internet, *Online Information 2001: proceedings*, Oxford, Learned Information, 17–23.

Handy, C. (1984) *The Future of Work: a guide to a changing society*, Oxford, Blackwell, ISBN 0855206888 (cased), 0855206896 (paperback).

Handy, C. (1995) *Beyond Certainty: the changing world of organisations*, London, Hutchinson, ISBN 0091791537 (Also Arrow, 1996, 0099549913).

Internet Society (1997) Available at http://alis.isoc.org/palmares.en.html [accessed 27 May 2003].

Librarians in the 21st century. Available at http://istweb.syr.edu/21stcenlib/ [accessed 7 May 2003].
    This site was created during the Spring 2000 semester by a class of graduate students in the Master of Library Science program in the School of Information Studies at Syracuse University, Syracuse, New York. Their assignment was to create an information resource for the world wide web that explored the nature of librarianship at the opening of the 21st century, looking at the current state of the profession and some directions in which it is likely to evolve.

Marfleet, J. and Kelly, C. (1999) Leading the Field: the role of the information professional in the next century, *The Electronic Library*, **17** (6), (December), 359–64.

Nunberg, G. (2000) Will the Web always Speak English? *American Prospect*, **11**(10), 27 March–10 April . Available at www.prospect.org/print-friendly/print/V11/10/nunberg-g.html [accessed 13 April 2003].

Pantry, S. and Griffiths, P. (1998) *Becoming a Successful Intrapreneur: a practical guide to creating an innovative information service*, London, Library Association Publishing, ISBN 1 85604 292 8.

Pantry, S. and Griffiths, P. (2001) *The Complete Guide to Preparing and*

Implementing Service Level Agreements, 2nd edn, London, Library Association Publishing, ISBN 1 85604 410 6.

Pimienta, D. (2000) Put Out Your Tongue and Say 'Aaah': is the internet suffering from acute 'Englishitis'? *Points of View*, 30 January. Available at ww.unesco.org/webworld/points_of_views/300102_pimienta.shtml/.

Rurak, M. (1998) Demand Explodes for Librarians with High-tech Research Skills, *National Business Employment Weekly*, August 25. Available at www.careerjournal.com/salaries/industries/librarians/19980825-rurak.html [accessed 27 May 2003].

Rosenfeld, L. and Morville, P. (2002) *Information Architecture for the World Wide Web*, 2nd edn, Cambridge MA, O'Reilly & Associates, ISBN 0596000359.

Simmons-Welburn, J. (2002) *Changing Roles of Library Professionals: executive report*, Washington, DC, Association of Research Libraries.

Thorhauge, J., Larsen, G., Thun, H.-P., Albrechtsen, H. and Segbert, M. (eds) (1997) *Public Libraries and the Information Society*, Luxembourg, Office for Official Publications of the European Communities, EUR 17648 EN, ISBN 9282805050.

Wilder, S. (2000) The Changing Profile of Research Library Professional Staff, *LA Bimonthly Report on Research Library Issues and Actions from ARL, CNI, and SPARC*, 208/209 (February/April), 4. Available at www.arl.org/newsltr/208_209/chgprofile.html/ [accessed 5 May 2003].

Wurman, R. S. (1989) *Information Anxiety*, New York, Doubleday.

Wurman, R. S., Sume, J. and Leifer, L. (2000) *Information Anxiey 2*, Indianapolis, Que.

Chapter 2 Your master career plan, or, Do you have to kiss a lot of frogs to find a prince or princess?

Aslib Directory of Information Sources in the United Kingdom (2002), 12th edn, London, Aslib/Europa Books and Directories, ISBN 0851424724. Available at www.europapublications.co.uk.

Bradley, P (2002) *Getting and Staying Noticed on the Web: your web promotion questions answered*, London, Facet Publishing, ISBN 1856044556.

CBD Research Ltd, Chancery House,15 Wickham Road, Beckenham, Kent BR3 5JS, UK. Tel: +44 (0)20 8650 7745; fax: +44 (0)20 8650 0768 has the following titles:

Centres, Bureaux and Research Institutes (2000) 4th edn, 2000, ISBN 0900246855.

Councils, Committees & Boards including Government Agencies and Authorities (2001) 12th edn, ISBN 0900246871.

Current European Directories (1994) 3rd edn, ISBN 0900246642.

Directory of British Associations and Associations in Ireland (2002) 16th edn, ISBN 0900246928.

Directory of European Industrial and Trade Associations (1997) 6th edn, ISBN 090024674X.

Directory of European Professional & Learned Societies (1995) 5th edn, ISBN 0900246707.

Pan-European Associations (1996) 3rd edn, ISBN 0900246731.

Guides to sources of company information:

American Companies Guide (1997) ISBN 0900246685.

Asian & Australian Companies Guide (1993) ISBN 0900246618.

European Companies Guide (1992) 4th edn, ISBN 0900246448.

Check the website www.cbdresearch.com for new editions.

CILIP: the Chartered Institute of Library and Information Professionals (2003) Portfolio Careers, CILIP, *Library and Information Appointments*, **6** (8), 11 April.

Competencies for Special Librarians of the 21st Century (1996) Special Libraries Association. Special Committee on Competencies for Special Librarians, *Competencies for Special Librarians of the 21st Century: full report*, submitted to the SLA Board of Directors by Joanne Marshall, Chair; Bill Fisher; Lynda Moulton; and Robert Piccoli, Washington, DC, SLA. Available at www.sla.org/content/SLA/professional/meaning.competency.cfm. [Accessed 20 April 2003]. See also Spiegelman, B. M., below.

Dale, P. and Wilson, P. (2003) *Guide to Libraries and Information Units in Government Departments and Other Organisations*, 34th edn, London, British Library (to be published January 2004 in North America), ISBN 0712308830.

Encyclopaedia of Associations: international organizations, London, Thomson Learning. Available at www.gale.com.

European Commission DGXIII EUROIEMASTERS project brochure. Available from the European Commission DGXIII/E-4, Euroforum, 10 Rue Robert Stumper, L-2557 Luxembourg. Tel: +353 4301 34195; fax: +352 4301 38069.

Gorman, G. E. and Clayton, P. (1997) *Qualitative Research for the Information Professional: a practical handbook*, London, Facet Publishing, ISBN 185041786. 2nd edition due early 2004, ISBN 1856044726.

Griffiths, P. (2000) *Managing Your Internet and Intranet Services: the information professional's guide to strategy*, London, Library Association Publishing, ISBN 1856043401 (2nd edn due 2003).

Hayes, J. E. and Todaro, J. (2000) *Careers in Libraries: a bibliography of traditional and web-based library career resources*, American Library Association. Available at www.ala.org/Content/NavigationMenu/ Our_Association/ Offices/Human_Resource_Development_and_Recruitment/Careers_in_ Libraries1/Careers_in_Libraries__A_Bibliography_of_Traditional_and_ Web-based_Library_Career_Resources.htm [accessed 7 May 2003].

Lewis, N. (1999) Level 4 NVQs: an alternative route to professional status?, *Library Association Record*, **101** (2), (February) , 94–6.

Libraries and Information Services in the United Kingdom and the Republic of Ireland 2003 (2002), 29th edn, London, Facet Publishing, ISBN 1856044505. Annual.

Meyriat, J. (1998) [Presentation of the European Project DECID: development of Eurocompetences for information and documentation], *IDT98 – Textes des Communications,* Paris, IDT/Jouve, 199–204 [in French].

Moore, N. (2000) *How to do Research: the complete guide to designing and managing research projects*, London, Library Association Publishing, 3rd edn, ISBN 1856043584.

Sheldrick R. C. and Dewdney, P. (1998) *Communicating Professionally: a how-to-do-it manual for library applications*, London, Facet Publishing, 2nd edn, ISBN 1856043193.

Spiegelman, B. M. (ed.) (1997) *Competencies for Special Librarians of the 21st Century*, Washington, DC, Special Libraries Association.

Thackray, B. (1998) National Vocational Qualifications in Information and Library Services – how and why, *IDT98 – Textes des Communications*, Paris, IDT/Jouve, 180–7.

Times Higher Education Supplement (jobs, courses and conferences). Available at www.thes.co.uk.

United Kingdom (2003) Department for Culture, Media and Sport, *Framework for the Future: libraries, learning and information in the next decade*, London, DCMS.

Yearbook of International Organizations: a guide to global civil society networks (2002) Union of International Associations, Brussels, 39th edn, 2002/2003, 5 vols. in 6 parts, Munich, K. G. Saur, ISBN 3598244967.

Library and information recruitment agencies
See next chapter for addresses and websites.

Organizations and subject interest groups mentioned in the text
International Fire Information and Research Exchange (inFIRE). Available at www.wpi.edu/Academics/Library/InFire/.

UK Fire Information Group. Available at www.ukfig.org.uk.

Healthcare and medicine

For current details of British and international organizations, provided and updated by the British Library, see www.bl.uk/services/information/hgroups.html [accessed 7 May 2003].

Law

BIALL – the British and Irish Association of Law Librarians, The Administrator, 26 Myton Crescent, Warwick, Warwickshire CV34 6QA, UK. Available at www.biall.org.uk [accessed 7 May 2003].

Other organizations mentioned

British Council, Bridgewater House, 58 Whitworth Street, Manchester M1 6BB, UK; 10 Spring Gardens, London SW1A 2BN, UK. Available at www.britishcouncil.org [accessed 7 May 2003].

Chartered Institute of Library and Information Professionals (CILIP), 7 Ridgmount Street, London WC1E 7AE, UK. Available at www.cilip.org.uk.

European Bureau of Library, Information and Documentation Associations (EBLIDA). Available at www.eblida.org.

European Council of Information Associations (ECIA). Available at www.aslib.co.uk/ecia.

International Federation of Library Associations (IFLA), PO Box 95312, 2509 CH, The Hague, Netherlands. Available at www.ifla.org.

Special Libraries Association, 1700 Eighteenth Street, NW, Washington, DC 20009-2514, USA. Available at www.sla.org [accessed 7 May 2003].

US Department of Labor, Bureau of Labor Statistics, *Occupational Outlook Handbook*. Available at www.bls.gov.uk [accessed 30 April 2003].

Chapter 3 Starting your career

Where to Study in the UK: courses accredited by CILIP: the Chartered Institute of Library and Information Professionals

The accreditation process is primarily concerned with the course relevance to current and developing practice in librarianship and information science; after initial accreditation CILIP will visit regularly and the date of the next accreditation is to the right of the course details. Post-experience courses ask that candidates have previous library and information experience at a professional level. Contact admissions departments for full entry requirements and check the websites [all accessed 7 May 2003] for details of current and proposed courses.

ABERDEEN

Department of Information Management, Aberdeen Business School, The Robert Gordon University, Garthdee Road, Aberdeen AB10 7QE, UK. Tel: +44 (0)1224 263901; fax: +44 (0)1224 263939; e-mail: slis@rgu.ac.uk; www.rgu.ac.uk/schools/.

ABERYSTWYTH

Department of Information Studies, University of Wales Aberystwyth, Llanbadarn Fawr, Aberystwyth, Ceredigion SY23 3AS, UK. Tel: +44 (0)1970 622155; fax: +44 (0)1970 622190; e-mail: dils@aber.ac.uk; www.dis.aber.ac.uk.

BIRMINGHAM

School of English, Information and Culture, University of Central England in Birmingham, Franchise Street, Perry Barr, Birmingham B42 2SU, UK. Tel: +44 (0)121 331 5625; fax: +44 (0)121 331 5675; e-mail: sis@uce.ac.uk; www.cie.uce.ac.uk.

BRIGHTON

School of Computing, Mathematics and Information Services, University

of Brighton, Watts Building, Lewes Road, Moulsecoomb, Brighton BN2
4GJ, UK. Tel: +44 (0)1273 643500; fax: +44 (0) 1273 642405; e-mail:
p.g.b.enser@brighton.ac.uk; www.cmis.brighton.ac.uk.

BRISTOL

Graduate School of Education, University of Bristol, 8–10 Berkeley Square,
Clifton, Bristol BS8 1HH, UK. Tel: +44 (0)117 928 7147; fax: +44
(0)117 925 4975; e-mail: Cathy.Badley@bris.ac.uk;
www.bristol.ac.uk/education/ilm.

EDINBURGH

School of Social Sciences, Media and Communication, Queen Margaret
University College, Clerwood Terrace, Edinburgh EH12 8TS, UK.
Tel: +44 (0)131 317 3502; fax: +44 (0)131 316 4165;
e-mail: gmcmurdo@qmuc.ac.uk; www.qmced.ac.uk.

GLASGOW

Department of Computer and Information Science, Graduate School of
Informatics, The University of Strathclyde, Livingstone Tower, 26
Richmond Street, Glasgow G1 1XH, UK. Tel: +44 (0)141 548 3700
direct, +44 (0)141 552 4400 switchboard; fax: +44 (0)141 552 5330;
e-mail: secretary@cis.strath.ac.uk; www.cis.strath. ac.uk.

LEEDS

School of Information Management, Leeds Metropolitan University,
Priestley Hall, Beckett Park, Leeds, LS6 3QS, UK. Tel. +44 (0)113
283 2600 ext 7421 (enquiries), ext 3728 (admin); fax: +44 (0)113 283
7599; e-mail: l.bilby@lmu.ac.uk (undergraduate), c.rankin@lmu.ac.uk
(postgraduate); www.lmu.ac.uk/ics/im.

LIVERPOOL

Centre Information and Library Management Group, Liverpool Business

School, Liverpool John Moores University, John Foster Building, 98 Mount Pleasant, Liverpool L3 5UZ, UK. Contact: Janet Farrow, Tel: +44 (0)151 231 3596; fax: +44 (0)151 7070423; e-mail: j.farrrow@livjm.ac.uk; http://cwis.livjm.ac.uk/bus/cilm/.

LONDON

Department of Information Science, The City University, Northampton Square, London EC1V 0HB, UK. Tel: +44 (0)20 7477 8381 direct, +44 (0)20 7477 8000 switchboard; fax: +44 (0)20 7477 8584; e-mail: dis@city.ac.uk; www.soi.city.ac.uk.

LONDON

School of Information Management, Department of Applied Social Sciences, North London Campus, London Metropolitan University, Ladbroke House, 62–66 Highbury Grove, London N5 2AD, UK. Tel: +44 (0)20 7753 5032; e-mail: admissions.north@londonmet.ac.uk; www.londonmet.ac.uk.

LONDON

Thames Valley University, St Mary's Road, Ealing, London W5 5RF, UK. Tel: +44 (0)20 8579 5000; fax: +44 (0)20 8566 1353; e-mail: learning.advice@tvu.ac.uk; www.tvu.ac.uk.

LONDON

School of Library, Archive, and Information Studies, University College London, Gower Street, London WC1E 6BT, UK. Tel: +44 (0)20 7679 7204; fax: +44 (0)20 7383 0557; email: slais-enquiries@ucl.ac.uk; www.ucl.ac.uk/slais.

LOUGHBOROUGH

Department of Information Science, Loughborough University, Loughborough, Leicestershire LE11 3TU, UK. Tel: +44 (0)1509 223052 direct; fax: +44 (0)1509 223053; e-mail: h.l.rees@lboro.ac.uk; www.lboro.ac.uk/departments/ls/.

MANCHESTER

Department of Information and Communications, Manchester Metropolitan University, Geoffrey Manton Building, Rosamond Street West, off Oxford Road, Manchester M15 6LL, UK. Tel: +44 (0)161 247 6144 direct; fax: +44 (0)161 247 6351; e-mail: infcomms-hums@mmu.ac.uk; www.mmu.ac.uk/h-ss/dic/.

NEWCASTLE

Division of Information and Communication Studies, School of Informatics, Northumbria University, Lipman Building, Newcastle upon Tyne, NE1 8ST, UK. Tel: +44 (0)191 227 4917 direct; fax: +44 (0)191 227 3671; e-mail: il.admin@unn.ac.uk; www.ilm.unn.ac.uk.

SHEFFIELD

Department of Information Studies, The University of Sheffield, Western Bank, Sheffield S10 2TN, UK. Tel: +44 (0)114 222 2630 (enquiries); fax: +44 (0)114 278 0300 ; e-mail: dis@sheffield.ac.uk; www.shef.ac.uk/uni/academic/I-M/is/home.html.

CILIP: membership, careers and qualifications

CILIP: the Chartered Institute of Library and Information Professionals, 7 Ridgmount Street, London WC1E 7AE, UK. Tel: +44 (0)20 7255 0610; textphone: +44 (0) 20 7255 0505; fax: +44 (0)20 7255 0501; e-mail: careers@cilip.org.uk; www.cilip.org.uk.

Recruitment agencies

Aslib Library Information Recruitment Consultancy, Temple Chambers, 3–7 Temple Avenue, London EC4Y 0HP, UK. Tel: +44 (0)20 7583 8900; fax: +44 (0)20 7583 8297; www.aslib.com/recruit.

Birchs Consultancy, Warnford Court, 29 Throgmorton Street, London EC2N 2AT, UK. Tel: +44 (0)20 7588 5752; fax: +44 (0)20 7256 5501; e-mail: Birchscon@AOL.com.

Capita RAS, Innovation Court, New Street, Basingstoke, Hampshire RG21 7JB. Tel: +44 (0)1256 869555; fax: +44 (0)1256 383785; www. capitaras.co.uk.

Librarian vacancies in government departments and agencies are advertised on this website and in appropriate publications. However, not all government bodies use Capita RAS but place direct advertisements themselves, so this is not an exclusive route to these vacancies.

CILIP: the Chartered Institute of Library and Information Professionals *Yearbook* for details of all the branches and groups, etc. (Most public libraries should have a copy.)

CILIP *Library and Information Appointments*, which is issued fortnightly to members. CILIP, 7 Ridgmount Street, London WC1E 7AE. Tel: +44 (0)20 7255 0500; fax: +44 (0)20 7255 0501; www.cilip.org.uk.

CILIP LISJobNet (electronic version of *Library and Information Appointments*). Available at www.lisjobnet.org.uk.

Glen Recruitment, 18 Southampton Place, London WC1A 2AX, UK. Tel: +44 (0)20 7745 7245; fax: +44 (0)20 7745 7244; e-mail: info@ glenrecruitment.co.uk; www.glenrecruitment.co.uk.

Instant Library Recruitment, 104b St John Street, London EC1M 4EH, UK. Tel: +44 (0)20 7608 1414; fax: + 44 (0)20 7608 1038; e-mail: recruitment@instant-library.com; www.instant-library.com.

Intelligent Resources, The London Fruit & Wool Exchange, Brushfield Street, London E1 6EP, UK. Tel: +44 (0)20 7375 0085; fax: +44 (0)20 7375 0095; www.intelligentresources.com. (Researchers, corporate intelligence specialists and publishing.)

Libex: Bureau for International Library Staff Exchange. From March 2003 this service has moved from the University of Wales, its home for the last 20 years, to CILIP (see entry above – contact: Angela Frampton).

Sue Hill Recruitment and Services Ltd, Borough House, 80 Borough High

Street, London SE1 1LL, UK. Tel: +44 (0)20 7378 7068; fax: +44 (0)20 7378 6838; e-mail: jobs@suehill.com; www.suehill.com.

TFPL Recruitment, 17–18 Britton Street, London EC1M 5TL, UK. Tel: +44 (0)20 7251 5522; fax: +44 (0)20 7251 8318; e-mail: recruitment@tfpl.com; www.tfpl.com.

New areas of work for library and information professionals

Best-Nichols, B. (1997) Technologies Change Organizational and Occupational Structures: librarian, cybrarian, or ? In Ensor, P. (ed.), *The Cybrarian's Manual*, Chicago, London, American Library Association, 385–94.

Fisher, B. (1994) *Mentoring*, London, Library Association Publishing.

Non-traditional Jobs for Librarians (2000) *Librarians in the 21st Century*. Available at http://istweb.syr.edu/21stcenlib/where/nonlibrary.html [accessed 7 May 2003].

Weaver, Susanna (2000) Non-traditional Jobs for Special Librarians. In *Special Libraries Management Handbook: the basics*, Columbia, University of South Carolina College of Librarianship and Information Science. Available at www.libsci.sc.edu/bob/class/clis724/SpecialLibraries Handbook/non-traditional.htm [accessed 30 March 2003].

Web work

Rosenfeld, L. and Morville, P. (2002) *Information Architecture for the World Wide Web*, 2nd edn, Cambridge, MA, O'Reilly & Associates, ISBN 0596000359. Available at www.oreillynet.com.

The authors say: 'We've often found that our backgrounds in information science and librarianship have proven very useful in dealing with the relationships between pages and other elements that make up a whole [web] site. Librarians have a long history of organizing and providing access to information, and are trained to work with searching, browsing and indexing technologies. Forward-looking librarians (sometimes described as 'cybrarians') see that their expertise applies in new arenas far beyond the library walls' (p.19, 'Who's qualified to practice information architecture?').

Literacy

Bookstart. Available at www.bookstart.co.uk/professionals/library.html [accessed 30 March 2003].

Chartered Institute of Library and Information Professionals (2002) *Start with the Child*, London, CILIP. Available at www.cilip.org.uk/advocacy/startwiththechild [accessed 30 March 2003].

Douglas, J. (2002) Start with the Child, *Update*, **1** (9), (December). Available at www.cilip.org.uk/update/issues/dec02/article4dec.html [accessed 30 March 2003].

Sure Start. Available at www.surestart.gov.uk (accessed 30 March 2003).

Usher, K. (2002) A Snapshot of the U.K. with Reference to Children's Libraries and Literature. Paper to *68th IFLA Council and General Conference, Glasgow, 18–24 August, 2002*. Available at www.ifla.org/IV/ifla68/papers/147-092e.pdf [accessed 30 March 2003].

Subject specific librarianship
Medical informatics

Giuse, N. B. et al. (1997) Preparing Librarians to Meet the Challenges of Today's Health Care Environment, *Journal of the American Medical Informatics Association*, **4**, 57–67.

Greenes, R. A. and Shortliffe, E. H. (1990) Medical Informatics: an emerging academic discipline and institutional priority, *JAMA*, **263** (8), (23 February), 1114–20.

Hersh, W. (2002) Medical Informatics: a career for librarians, LISJobs.com (March). Available at www.lisjobs.com/newsletter/archives/mar02whersh.htm (accessed 30 March 2003).

Knowledge management

Davenport, T. H. and Prusak, L. (1998) *Working Knowledge: how organizations manage what they know*, Boston, MA, Harvard Business School Press; paperback (2000), ISBN 1578513014.

Competitive intelligence

Hutchinson, B. and Warren, M. (2001) *Information Warfare: corporate attack and defence in a digital world*, London, Butterworth-Heinemann.
Society of Competitive Intelligence Professionals (SCIP). Available at www.scip.org.ci [accessed 7 May 2003].

Overseas qualifications

Information available at www.cilip.org.uk/jobs_careers/overseas.html [accessed 7 May 2003].

Chapter 4 Applying for a job

Abell, A. and Stenson, A. (1998) Building up a Valuable Career, *CILIP Library and Information Appointments*, **1** (14), (3 July), 1–2.
CILIP: the Chartered Institute of Library and Information Professionals, Salary Guides. Available at www.cilip.org.uk/salaryguides and www.lisjobnet.org.uk/jobseek/salary.html.
Hill, S. J. (1995) Get that Job – an introduction, *Librarian Career Development*, **3** (1), 5–8.
Hill, S. J. (1993) Hints and Tips for Getting that Job, *Librarian Career Development*, **1** (2), 31–2.

Job opportunities

If you are interested in working in other countries, the listing below will provide assistance in your search for further information [websites accessed 7 May 2003].

- Contact the country's representative in the UK to find out about required work permits and visas. For contact details consult Whitaker's Almanack or search the internet. The UK Foreign and Commonwealth Office's website contains a lot of useful country information and advice. See www.fco.gov.uk/ under Travel Advice, or tel: +44 (0)20 7270 1500.
- You will need to ensure that your qualifications transfer overseas. To find out more, send the exact title of the award, date and place obtained to CILIP's Qualifications Department: tel: +44 (0)20 7255 0610; e-mail: quals@cilip.org.uk.
- For more information on the country you wish to visit contact the local British Council office. The British Council's various locations can be found on the internet at www.britishcouncil.org or through their general enquiries line at tel: +44 (0)161 957 7755; fax +44 (0)161 957 7762; e-mail: general.enquiries@britishcouncil.org.
- Information on employment opportunities, salary scales and status of library and information workers within your country of interest may be obtainable from the local library and information association. Please note, however, that the level of information given will vary depending on the resources available in the local organization. Some of these organizations can be found on the American Library Association's website at www.ala.org/work/international/associations.html, but this list is not comprehensive. Another source is the *IFLA Membership Directory*, available at www.ifla.org/III/members/index.htm, or contact CILIP, which can provide contact details for those organizations without a web presence.
- For library and information posts overseas scan *Library and Information Appointments*, free with your CILIP membership. This service is also

available on the internet and you can search by sector, location and salary band. Available at www.lisjobnet.org.uk.

- If you are interested in voluntary work contact Voluntary Service Overseas (VSO) if you are available for at least two years: VSO, 317 Putney Bridge Road, London SW15 2PN, UK. E-mail: enquiry@vso.org.uk; www.vso.org.uk. Your CILIP membership fee will be waived for the time you volunteer abroad.

- For more experienced professionals register with British Executive Service Overseas (BESO): 164 Vauxhall Bridge Road, London, SW15 2PN, UK. E-mail: registrar@BESO.org; www.beso.org.

- Consider subscribing to *Overseas Job Express*, a regular newspaper of international job opportunities: 3rd floor, 20 New Road, Brighton BN1 1UF, UK. Tel: +44 (0)1273 699777; fax: +44 (0)1273 699778; e-mail: info@overseasjobsexpress.co.uk; www.overseasjobsexpress.com/ Home.htm.

- Subscribe to IFLA's LIBJOBS mailing list. To subscribe and receive job postings send the message 'subscribe LIBJOBS [your name]' to ifla. listserv@infoserv.inist.fr. Access is also available through www.ifla.org/II/lists/libjobs.htm.

- DfES has a useful website, which provides information on the rights and requirements for people with professional qualifications gained in one EU member state who wish to work in another member state. It includes links to the websites of designated authorities, including CILIP. Available at www.dfes.gov.uk/europeopen.

- Consider contacting Careers Europe, a UK resource centre with information on careers within the EU: Careers Europe, 3rd floor, Midland House, 14 Cheapside, Bradford BD1 4JA, UK. Tel: +44 (0)1274 829600; fax: +44 (0)1274 829610; www.careerseurope.co.uk/.

- *The Riley Guide: employment opportunities and job resources on the internet*, compiled by M. F. Dikel. Available at www.rileyguide.com. This USA-based site includes: Prepare for a Job Search; Resumes & Cover Letters, Targeting & Researching Employers, etc.; Executing Your Job Search

Campaign; Job Listings!; Networking, Interviewing & Negotiating; Salary Guides & Guidance Information for Recruiters. There is relevant background and some non-US resources are also listed.

- For information about opportunities in the United States see the American Library Association's revised website at www.ala.org/Content/Navigation Menu/Education_and_Careers/Employment_Opportunities/Employment _Opportunities.htm [accessed 7 May 2003] and Moore, M. (2003) *Guide to Employment Sources in the Library and Information Professions*, ALA. Available at www.ala.org/Content/NavigationMenu/Our_Association/Offices/ Human_Resource_Development_and_Recruitment/Library_Employment _Resources/Guide_to_Employment_Sources_in_the_Library_and_ Information_Profession.htm [accessed 7 May 2003].

See also the recruitment agencies listed in Chapter 3.

Chapter 5 Next steps in your career, including promotion plans

Abell, A. and Stenson, A. (1998) Building up a Valuable Career, *Library and Information Appointments*, 1 (14), (3 July), 1–2.

Dalton, P, Mynott, G, and Shoolbred, M. (2000) Barriers to Career Development within the LIS Profession, *Library review*, **49** (6), 271–6.

Stretton, V and King, L. (2003) Know Where you Stand, *Information World Review*, **190**, (April), 22–3.

Mentoring

Brewerton, A. (2002) Mentoring, *SCONUL Newsletter*, (Spring), 21–30.

Brewerton, A. and Cipkin, C. (2001) Dial M for Mentor, *Library and Information Appointments*, **4** (19), (7 September), 469–70.

Nankivell, C. and Shoolbred, M. (1997) Mentoring: a valuable tool for career development, *Librarian Career Development*, **5** (3), 98–104.

Smith, A. and Morgan, S. (2001) Informal Mentoring: a perspective from both sides, *SCONUL Newsletter*, **24**, (Winter), 25–8.

Chapter 6 Your successful interview

Goleman, D. (2000) *Working with Emotional Intelligence*, New York, Bantam Doubleday Dell, ISBN 0553378589. Or you can try out some EQ tests at www.queendom.com/tests/iq/emotional_iq.html.

Gottesman, D. and Mauro, B. (1999) *The Interview Rehearsal Book: 7 steps to job-winning interviews using acting skills you never knew you had*, New York, Berkeley Pub. Group, ISBN 0425166864.

Hackett, P. (1998) *The Selection Interview*, London, CIPD Publishing, ISBN 0852927568.

Hill, S. J. (1993) Hints and Tips for Getting that Job, *Librarian Career Development*, **1** (2), 31–2.

Hill, S. J. (1995) Get that Job – an introduction, *Librarian Career Development*, **3** (1), 5–8.

Hill, S. J. (1996) Get that Job – interviews, *Librarian Career Development*, **4** (1), 33–6.

Lines, J. (1997) *30 Minutes – before a job interview*, London, Kogan Page, ISBN 0749423684.

Pease, A. (1999) *Body Language*, Oxford, Butterworth-Heinemann, ISBN 9971643588.

After the interview, if you don't get the job, consult these sites [accessed 7 May 2003]: www.collegegrad.com; www.acetheinterview.com.

Dress and appearance

Bounds, W. and Lublin, J. S. (1998) Appearance Still Matters Despite Casual Dress Codes, *Wall Street Journal*, (29 July).

Cartoon (1999) Cartoon Ties the Limit for Businesswomen, *Times*, (1 January), 3.

Colour me Professional. *BBC News*. Available at http://news.bbc.co.uk/1/hi/business/1500328.stm. (Includes details of a survey that recommends the best colours to wear to interview.)

First impressions (2000) *Library and Information Appointments*, **5** (18), (16 August) and **5** (20) (27 September). (Guidance on the first impression at interview.)

Sampson, E., Williams, L. and Lines, J. (2001) *The 30-minute Career Kit*, London, Kogan Page. A boxed set of four titles from Kogan Page's '30-minute' series including *30 minutes – before a job interview* (see above).

Chapter 7 After the interview

Stein, M. (2001) *Fearless Interviewing: what to do before, during and after the interview,* Lincoln, NE, iUniverse.com, ISBN 059519298X.

Also check out www.collegegrad.com and www.acetheinterview.com for job search information and advice (both accessed May 2003).

Chapter 8 Looking sideways . . . and back

Dewar, D. (1998) Shock Tactics for the Job Jungle, *Library Association Record,* **100** (12), (December), 651.

Griffiths, P. and MacLachlan, E. A. (1987) Library Consultancy in the Foreign and Commonwealth Office and the Overseas Development Administration, *Program,* **21** (2), 91–107.

Hannabus, S. (1998) Flexible Jobs: changing patterns in information and library work, *New Library World,* **99** (141), 104–11.

Liberman, S. (2002) How to be a Top Temp, *CILIP Library and Information Appointments,* (7 June), **5** (12), 1–2.

McIver, C. (1986) Use and Abuse of Consultants, *Management Today*, (February), 72–4.

Weaver-Mayers, R. (1994) If You Can't Go . . . Grow!, papers presented at the ALA Annual Conference, New Orleans, 1993, *Library Administration Management*, **9** (1), 12–26. Practical ways to cope with a career plateau.

Chapter 9 Other considerations in career planning

Biddiscombe, R. (1997) *Training for IT,* London, Library Association Publishing, ISBN 1856041867.

Foster, A. (1998) Knowing the Business: knowledge professionals need more than information skills, *Information World Review*, (November), 42.

Goulding, A. and Kerslake, E. (1997) *Training for Part-time and Temporary Workers*, London, Library Association Publishing, ISBN 1856042421.

Hornby, S. and Clarke, Z. (2002) *Challenge and Change in the Information Society*, London, Facet Publishing, ISBN 185604453X.

Lacey Bryant, S. (1995) *Personal Professional Development and the Solo Librarian,* London, Library Association Publishing, ISBN 1856041417.

Morris, B. (1993) *Training and Development for Women*, London, Library Association Publishing, ISBN 1856040801.

Owen, T. B. (2003) *Success at the Enquiry Desk*, 4th rev. edn, London, Facet Publishing, ISBN 1856044777.

Pantry, S. and Griffiths, P. (1998) *Becoming a Successful Intrapreneur: a practical guide to creating an innovative information service*, London, Library Association Publishing, ISBN 1856042928.

Stewart, A. (1996) Preparing for re-entry, *Library Association Record,* **98** (10), (October), 522–3. (Returning to work after a career break.)

Chapter 10 Case studies

Pat Gallaher

Gallaher, P. E. (1990) Public Library Services, with Emphasis on Country Areas, *Western Perspectives: Library and Information Services in Western Australia*, Perth, ALIA.

Gallaher, P. E. (1990) Libraries in Western Australia: the North, In *Conference Proceedings, Vol 1, ALIA 1st Biennial Conference*, Perth.

Sharr, F. A.(1992) *Recollections: forty years of public library service*, Adelaide, Auslib Press.

Irja Laamenan

Forty articles, of which four on genetics and the rest on chemical safety data and databases and informatics. Two posters presented in the ICOH conferences (Singapore 2000 and Brazil 2003).

Co-author:

Riihimäki, V., Isotalo, L., Jauhiainen, M., Kemiläinen, B., Laamanen, I., Luotamo, M., Riala, R. and Zitting, A. (2002) *Kemikaaliturvallisuuden Tiedonlähteet*, Helsinki, Työterveyslaitos. Also available at www.occuphealth. fi/ttl/osasto/tt/Kemikaalitieto/index.html. [Accessed 24 April 2003]

Tieto ja Tekniikka – Missä on Nainen? (2002) Various authors and editors include: Smeds, R., Kauppinen, K., Yrjänheikki, K. and Valtonen, A. Helsinki, Tekniikan Akateemisten Liitto TEK. ISBN 952-5005-67-4.

Den Tredje Nordiska Konferensen för Medicinska Bibliotekarier, Helsingfors 26.-28.8.1991: föredrag och sammandrag av paneldiskussionen och gruppmötena (1992) Compilers: Laamanen, I., Luoma, A., Salmi, L., Helsinki, Bibliothecarii Medicinae Fenniae.

Index